MW01241969

CORPORATE
INNOVATION

A Baldrige-based Assessment
of Innovative Corporate Practices
and Entrepreneurship

Other books by the author:

Corporate University: A Baldrige-based Assessment for the 21st-Century Workforce

Corporate Intelligence: A Baldrige-based Corporate Espionage Organizational Assessment

Corporate Sustainability Planning Assessment Guide: A Comprehensive Organizational Assessment
    (Global Reporting Initiative [GRI] Index Included)

Homeland Security Assessment Manual: A Comprehensive Organizational Assessment based on Baldrige Criteria

Baldrige on Campus: The Assessment Workbook for Higher Education

The Simplified Baldrige Award Organization Assessment

Measuring Up to The Baldrige: A Quick and Easy Self-Assessment Guide for Companies of All Sizes

The Baldrige Workbook for Healthcare

Demystifying Baldrige

Published by CreateSpace – an Amazon Company

Inquiries should be addressed to:

Permissions Department
MSQPC–The Quality Center
22 N. Front Street, Suite 200
Memphis, TN 38103

ISBN-13: 978-1533196897
ISBN-10: 1533196893

1. Total quality management - United States - Handbooks, manuals, etc.
2. Malcolm Baldrige National Quality Award. I. Fisher, Donald C.

Cover design by Latrescia Goss

Contents

I dedicate this book to my mother
Robbie Cruse Fisher,
who has practiced Innovation
and Entrepreneurship for 91 years.

Foreword

In April 2016, leaders of the U.S. Department of Commerce recognized the 2015 recipients of the prestigious Malcolm Baldrige National Quality Award, which is looked upon as the nation's highest honor for organizational and performance excellence. The recipients shared best practices and various approaches taken by their team members to demonstrate role model processes required to attain outstanding business results, regardless of size, scope, industry, internal challenges, or external forces.

While working in the Service industry for more than 30 years and serving as a National Baldrige Examiner, Team Lead, and Judge, I have personally witnessed the positive impact of innovation, visionary leadership, and best practices on organizations across America. It is because of these testimonials, observations, and visions of future success stories that I express the significance of reading publications that are offered by Donald C. Fisher, Ph.D. I have known Dr. Fisher for several years now, worked with him on multiple projects in Memphis, Tennessee, and have always been intrigued with his commitment to supporting organizations in their pursuit of Performance Excellence or process improvement.

In his latest publication, Corporate Innovation, A Baldrige-based Assessment of Innovative Corporate Practices and Entrepreneurship; Dr. Fisher shares with readers the historical role, and breakthrough impact that innovation had and continues to have on corporations ability to sustain its effectiveness in the global marketplace. He explores the ongoing need for innovation to shape the "new" landscape for the American culture and the requirement for corporations to foster a culture that embraces the creative and innovative ideas of employees at all levels of the organization.

Dr. Fisher has a long-standing reputation for his advocacy of the Baldrige Framework, his many contributions to the Baldrige process as an Examiner and Judge, and his leadership through quality training. Over the years, he has interviewed countless business leaders to gain insight and perspective into their approaches for sustaining organizations. His work is well-documented and this latest publication on Corporate Innovation, may serve as the catalyst that help encourage corporate leaders to analyze their organization with a new set of lenses; the Baldrige Performance Excellence Framework.

Michael L. Dockery, MBA
National Judge - Malcolm Baldrige National Quality Award Program
Senior Manager, FedEx Express
Memphis, TN

Preface

Innovation is the key to growth and competitiveness for the 21st century organization. The benefit of innovation for both the organization at the corporate level and the economy at the national and global level is undeniable. Innovation involves adopting an idea, process, technology, product or business model that is either new or new to its proposed application.

The outcome of innovation is a "breakthrough" change in results, products, or processes. Innovation benefits from a supportive senior management environment which allows for intelligent risk taking and helps an organization identify strategic opportunities and promotes knowledge sharing among many disciplines. New products, processes and services which allow an organization to reduce its development/production costs, access new markets or develop new pathways of doing things opens up many windows of opportunity.

Innovation within organization's has opened up unlimited creative idea sharing among employees at all levels and provided solutions to new and better ways of resolving age old organizational problems. It has allowed the workforce to be creative and "think out of the Box" and to expand their vision and problem solving skills and abilities far beyond the confronts of traditional organizational problem solving techniques. Weather its breakthrough improvement or a change in approach regarding the organization's structure or business model innovation can lead an organization into an expanded market share to a leaner organization that works more effectively, efficiently and is more focused on results.

Innovation is a tool for entrepreneurs to use to create new and/or improved products/services for organizations. The new products/services may exploit an established technology or it may be the radical outcome of a whole new technology never before realized as a resolution to a problem. Innovation is the translation of an idea into an application. It requires ingenuity, creativity, enterprise, imagination, forward thinking and persistence in analytically working out the details of the product/service design and to develop the marketing, obtain finances, plan operations and distribution channels.

In a global economy that is driven by innovative practices and entrepreneurs that exploit change as an opportunity for a different business or a different service it is imperative that organizations assess their internal sources of innovative corporate practices and entrepreneurship. This comprehensive manual will aid and expedite an organization's corporate innovation efforts by identifying strengths and opportunities for improvement regarding mature and emerging innovative and entrepreneurial practices. This manual will also be most valuable in developing, revising, and/or improving an organizations innovative and entrepreneurial efforts through an overall organizational assessment and the ultimate development of a Corporate Innovation Plan.

Introduction

INNOVATION is what globalization has always been about. "We live in a world dominated by innovative Companies like Amazon, Apple, Samsung, Toyota, Tesla, Microsoft, Alphabet (Google), Twitter and Facebook. And even in the face of a recession, Silicon Valley's relentless entrepreneurs have continued to churn out start-up companies with outsize, world-changing ambitions." [1]

"Innovations that expand the human intellect and its creative, expressive and even moral possibilities includes the printing press, paper, the internet, the personal computer, semiconductor electronics and photography. Innovations that are integral to the physical and operating infrastructure of the modern world include cement, electricity, sanitation systems, pasteurization and air-conditioning. Innovations that enabled the Industrial Revolution and its successive waves include the steam engine, industrial steelmaking, refining, drilling of oil, nitrogen fixation, green revolution, moldboard ploy, Archimedes screw, scientific plant breeding, penicillin, vaccination, the pill, sanitation systems, and refrigeration. Innovations that allowed real-time communication beyond the range of a single human voice include the internet, telegraph, telephone, radio, and television. Innovations in the physical movement of people and goods include the internal combustion engine, automobile, airplane, steam engine, sailboat, sextant, compass and rocketry. Organizational breakthroughs include the Gregorian calendar, and alphabetization. Innovations for warfare included gunpowder and nuclear fission." [2]

11 Innovations that Changed the World

Innovations have always been the major catalysts behind expanding the human experience. Some of the breakthroughs brought about immediate change, while others laid the groundwork for important developments for the future. From pioneering inventions to bold scientific and medical advancements that have changed the course of human history the following are major innovations that laid the foundation for today's human exploration.[3] The 11 innovations that changed history include:

1. **The Printing Press** – Democratization of knowledge
2. **The Compass** – Impacted early navigation and exploration
3. **Paper Currency** – Changed the face of global economics
4. **Steel** – Fueled the Industrial Revolution and built modern cities
5. **Electric Light** – Liberated society from total reliance on daylight
6. **Domestication of the Horse** – Enabled travel and trade
7. **Transistors** – Provided the Elemental piece of electronic circuitry
8. **Magnifying Lenses** – Led to breakthrough in visual technology
9. **The Telegraph** – Transformed and expanded communications
10. **Antibiotics** - Combated bacteria
11. **The Steam Engine** – Provided energy in motion [4]

Bell Labs and Innovation

"Since Bell Laboratories (also known as Bell Labs and formerly named AT&T Bell Laboratories and Bell Telephone Laboratories) is a research and scientific development company that now belongs to Nokia. Its headquarters are located in Murray Hill, New Jersey, in addition to other laboratories around the rest of the United States and in other countries. Bell Labs opened its doors in 1925, and has been consistently tasked with solving difficult industrial problems. In 1925, Western Electric Research Laboratories and part of the engineering department of the American Telephone & Telegraph Company (AT&T) were consolidated to form Bell Telephone Laboratories, Inc., as a separate entity. At its peak, Bell Laboratories was the premier facility of its type, developing a wide range of revolutionary technologies, including the development of radio astronomy, the transistor, the laser, the charge-coupled device (CCD), information theory, the UNIX operating system and the programming languages C, C++, and S, Eight Nobel Prizes have been awarded for work completed at Bell Laboratories." [5]

"In the beginning Bell Labs was populated with physics, engineering and chemistry grad students and junior professors seduced away from colleges with better pay. The new recruits were required to climb telephone poles, operate a switchboard, and sign a paper that sold all rights to any future patents to AT&T for a dollar. Bell Labs was a place for discovery, which was not always profitable. During World War II, the U.S. government invested $2 billion into the development of the atomic bomb, but they invested around $3 billion in the development of radar, much of which took place at Bell Labs. During the post-war reorganization of Bell Labs, older management was demoted, younger management given new titles, and every research group was interdisciplinary. Chemists mingled with physicists who chatted with metallurgist who lunched with engineers. Every building on the Bell Labs New Jersey campus was interconnected and no one was allowed to shut their door. This was the beginning a newly innovative time for Bell Labs." [6]

"The story of the idea factory, as Bell Labs was referenced in Jon Gertner's book The Idea Factory Bell Labs and the Great Age of American Innovation. He noted that Bell Labs included a world of fascinating, brilliant people and the challenges that they overcame in developing amazing technological achievements." [7] Five elements that Gertner listed which set the foundation and were critical for Bell Labs' success in innovation that other organizations' should consider include:

1. **Inhibit a problem-rich environment** – Organizations' to solve customer needs and not become internally focused on their own problems.

2. **Cognitive diversity gets breakthroughs** – Bell Labs were deliberately stocked with scientists from different disciplines. The intention was to bring together people with different perspectives and knowledge to innovate on the problems they want solved.

3. **Expertise and HiPPOs derail innovation** – What makes wrong predictions even more harmful is the position of the person who makes them. Experts are granted greater license to determine the feasibility and value of an idea. HiPPOs (high paid person's opinion) are granted similar vaunted positions. In both cases, their positions when they get it wrong can undermine innovation.

4. **Experiment and learn when it comes to new ideas** – Start with an experiment. "There's a difference, you see, in thinking idly about something, and in setting out to do something".

5. **Innovation can sow the seeds of one's own destruction** – Even patented innovations will find substitute methodologies emerging to compete. This fits a common meme, that ideas are worthless, and execution is everything. It is also seen in the dynamic of the first-to-market firm losing the market by subsequent entrants. After the innovation, relentless execution is the key to winning the market.[8]

The Future of Corporate Innovation and Entrepreneurship

Most large corporations' understand the need to build an organization that can deal with the ever increasing forces of a global recession and continuous disruption and the need for continuous innovation, globalization and regulation. "There is no standard strategy and structure for creating corporate innovation. According to Steve Blank, a Silicon Valley entrepreneur and academician, collectively we are beginning to see a pattern regarding some concrete suggestions about Corporate Management and Innovation strategy and the structural changes corporations need to make in order to cultivate an innovative workforce. Blank notes that while companies have existed for the last 400 years, their modern form is less than 150 years old. In the U.S. the growth of railroads, telegraph, meat packers, steel and industrial equipment forced companies to deal with strategies of how to organize a complex organization. This strategy forced companies to be structured around functions such as manufacturing, purchasing, or sales. 90 years ago companies faced new strategic pressures as physical distances in the United States limited their daily hands-on-management in addition to managing diverse product lines. In the 1920's, companies restructured from monolithic functional organizations by sales, marketing, manufacturing, and purchasing, and reorganized into operating divisions by product, territory, or brand each with its own profit and loss responsibility. This strategy to structure shifted from functional organizations to operating divisions led by DuPont and popularized by General Motors and quickly followed by Standard Oil and Sears." [9]

"A new strategy for entrepreneurship in the 21st century corporation goes beyond focusing on improving existing business models to inventing new business models that require entirely new organizational structures and skills. Companies have found that their existing strategy and structures are inadequate to respond to a changing world." [10] Steve Blank, in his blog entitled "The Future of Corporate Innovation and Entrepreneurship" states that corporations equipped for the challenges of the 21st Century think of innovation as a sliding scale between execution and search."[11]

He lists the following considerations for organizations to consider:

1. For companies to survive in the 21st Century they need to continually create a new set of businesses, by inventing new business models.

2. Most of these new businesses need to be created outside of the existing business units.

3. The exact form of the new business models is not known at the beginning. It only emerges after an intense business model design and search activity based on the customer development process.

4. Companies will have to maintain a portfolio of new business model initiatives, not unlike a venture capital firm, and they will have to accept that maybe only 1 out of 10 initiatives might succeed.

5. To develop this new portfolio, companies need to provide a stable innovation funding mechanism for a new business creation, one that is simply thought of as a cost of doing business.

6. Many of the operating divisions can and should provide resources to the new businesses inside the company.

7. A new organizational structure needs to be developed to manage the creation of new businesses and to coordinate the sharing of business model resources.

8. Some of these new businesses might become new resources to the existing operating units in the company or they could grow into becoming the new profit generating business units of the company's future.[12]

Rewarding Innovation

The American Productivity & Quality Center (APQC) in Houston, Texas has found that organizations need innovative approaches to rewards and recognition to drive innovation in products and services. Employees have valid needs for achievement, status, and affiliation, and organizations are tasked with providing structure and consistency in motivating the workforce to pursue creative and innovative ideas.[13]

APQC has outlined the basics that leading organizations have used to drive innovation among the workforce through rewards and recognition. They include the following:

- Create a design team.

- Consistently acknowledge those who contribute ideas, knowledge, and time. Senior management may recognize innovative design teams and champions, whereas peers typically nominate and recognize teammates for their contributions to the overall effort.

- Provide special recognition to volunteers, change agents, and model innovators. Keep names associated with contributions.

- Disseminate success stories concerning invention of a successful new product or approach.

- Make innovation self-rewarding. Being perceived as an expert by peers and management matters.

- Link innovation to the core cultural values of the organization. Explain the justification behind rewards and how meeting goals will affect overall and individual outcomes.

- Compile a committee of human resources, knowledge management, research and development, and representatives from business units to develop guidelines and suggestions to encourage innovation.[14]

Building a Culture of Innovation

"Original corporations that governed by the tea trade in India and England or more modern corporations like the U.S. automobile companies or banks, the prevailing wisdom has been to grow large and use size, mass and reach to defeat other competitors. By growing large organizations costs are distributed more effectively; they serve more customers from the same basic set of products, scale revenues and introduce efficiencies and common market power and dominate sales channels. In a market where size matters, only a few players dominate and the rest compete for the leftovers. Large companies become defensive, complacent and inert, held in place by investments and past performance, and are overly risk averse. Their size and their business model ultimately become a barrier for new innovation and new growth. An example would be Sears once the largest retailer in the world that actually made a significant transition from a catalog company (In many respects the world's first Amazon) to a company that based its model on stores in shopping malls. Sears is locked into a business model that is exceptionally difficult to change. What was a once promising model is now driving Sears toward a disaster." [15]

"The J. C. Penny Company's experience was about an organization that tried to innovate their business model to include more upscale clothing and to eliminate coupons and discounting. That experiment lasted less than two years before Penney's brought back its former management team. Lessons to be learned from the Penny's experiment is that Innovation is something every company should be constantly experimenting with, and communicating to its employees and customers why these experiments are taking place and what changes they are expecting and planning to implement. In Penney's case, there lack of overall stakeholder involvement, experimentation, and buy-in before the corporate-wide program was implemented." [16]

"Many organizations place a premium on helping their employees develop innovative ideas. Several notable examples include Alphabet (frequently informally referred to as Google), 3M, and Humana. Google notes that it is "passion, not perks" that fosters a culture of innovation. David Lawee, the company's vice president for corporate development, was quoted in the New York Times article as saying: At Google entrepreneurs "have to think bigger." The article noted that Google backs up their culture of innovation by providing resources, including infrastructure, money, time and people, "but most important a vision that tests most entrepreneurs to think bigger than they ever have before". Google has given its employees 20 percent of their time to work on pet projects, which is how Gmail and AdSense, two of the company's most successful products were developed. Similarly, 3M has allowed employees to spend 15 percent of their time on projects and research that go beyond their core responsibilities, in which, multilayer optical films and silicon adhesive systems for transdermal drug delivery were created. 3M prides itself as fostering a "Culture of Innovation" and also provides seed money of $30,000 to $75,000 called Genesis Grants to employees for developing ideas over a 12 month time period." [17] In 2013 Humana did benchmarking, competitive analysis, and site visits to other companies and determined that the innovation function at Humana needed to be able to do two things:

- Lead and drive transformational innovation for the company.
- Help the rest of the business innovate within their own means.[18]

The two primary types of innovation within Humana are transformational and incremental. Both are considered vital because incremental helps the company remain competitive, and it involves logical, timely extensions or modifications of current capabilities. "Transformational innovation is riskier and is exploratory by nature. It typically converts to new capabilities which Humana adopts and scales within their business." [19] Humana directly attributes the transformational and incremental concept to their future growth to what is seen as a significant business opportunity for the organization.[20]

About This Manual

This manual can be used to conduct a comprehensive Corporate Innovation Organizational Assessment based on the Baldrige Performance Excellence Framework. These guidelines for developing, evaluating or revising an existing Corporate Innovation Plan and/or developing a new plan, can provide a unique perspective regarding identifying various vulnerabilities and opportunities regarding innovation that exist within the overall corporate operations and infrastructure.

1 How to Assess Your Organization's Innovative Practices

The alignment of the Performance Excellence Criteria with corporate innovation planning provides a unique assessment methodology for an organization to gauge its innovative corporate practices and entrepreneurship. The Baldrige Criteria for Performance Excellence have been recognized as a "best practice" initiative for organizations to use to assess and to ensure that their corporate innovative practices are both sustainable and competitive in the global marketplace.

An organization would want to assess itself using the Performance Excellence Criteria because thousands of U.S. organizations stay abreast of ever-increasing competition and improve their overall performance using this internationally recognized quality standard. The Criteria can help an organization align resources and approaches and improve corporate-wide communications, productivity, and effectiveness as it relates to innovation.

The Corporate Innovation Assessment Scoring System is based on two evaluation dimensions: (1) process and (2) results. Each dimension should be considered before assigning a percentage score. All process evaluation dimension categories are linked to results and to each other. In addition, each of the categories assessed will have Corporate Innovation Scoring Profiles based on Sustainable Levels of Progression.

Process Evaluation Dimension (Categories 1-6)

"Process" refers to the methods your organization uses and improves to address the item requirements in Categories 1-6. The four factors used to evaluate process are approach, deployment, learning, and integration (A-D-L-I).

"Approach" (A) refers to:

- The methods used to accomplish the process
- The appropriateness of the methods to the item requirements
- The effectiveness of use of the methods
- The degree to which the approach is repeatable and based on reliable data and information (i.e., systematic)

"Deployment" (D) refers to the extent to which:

- Your approach is applied in addressing item requirements relevant and important to your organization
- Your approach is applied consistently
- Your approach is used by all appropriate work units

"Learning" (L) refers to:

- Refining your approach through cycles of evaluation and improvement
- Encouraging breakthrough change to your approach through innovation
- Sharing of refinements and innovation with other relevant work units and processes in your organization

"Integration" (I) refers to the extent to which:

- Your approach is aligned with your organizational needs identified in other criteria item requirements
- Your measures, information, and improvement systems are complementary across processes and work units
- Your plans, processes, results, analysis, learning, and actions are harmonized across processes and work units to support organization-wide goals.[21]

Results Evaluation Dimension (Category 7)

"Results" refers to your organization's outputs and outcomes in achieving the requirements in items 7.1-7.6. The five factors used to evaluate results are performance levels, trends, comparisons, linkage, and gap (Le-T-C-Li-G).

"Performance Levels" (Le) refers to:

- Performance position of data
- Rank of data performance
- Current data performance
- Numerical information that places or positions the organization's results and performance on a meaningful measurement scale

"Trends" (T) refers to:

- Ratio (i.e., slope of trend data)
- Breadth (i.e., how widely deployed and shared)

"Comparisons" (C) refers to:

- Performance relative to appropriate comparisons
- Comparisons against exemplary results

"Linkage" (Li) refers to:

- Alignment of data to important customer product and service, process, and action plan performance requirements
- Complementary measures and results that are aligned throughout many parts of the organization
- Connective measures throughout the organization that drive key organizational strategies and goals

"Gap" (G) refers to:

- An interval in results data
- Missing segments of data [22]

"Importance" as a Scoring Consideration

The two evaluation dimensions described in the previous sections are critical to evaluation and feedback. However, another critical consideration in evaluation and feedback is the importance of your reported process and results to your organization's key business factors (i.e., key student and other customer requirements, competitive environment, key strategic objectives, and action plans). [23]

The percent scores range from a low of 0% for zero-based preparation to a high of 100% for world-class preparation. An organization can be 0% (zero-based) in some areas and 100% (world-class) in others. The anchor point is 50%, which is middle range. Many organizations fall below the 50% anchor point regarding corporate innovation planning. The 50% anchor point is considered to be good, but certainly below what an organization that is striving to be "best-in-class" in corporate innovation preparation and progression would score when compared among leading organizations.

Organizations that score 0% have an anecdotal approach, lack deployment, and have no meaningful results. Organizations that score 100% reflect a refined, very mature approach that is deployed and well adapted with sustainable results in all relevant areas of the organization.

Scoring Profiles Based on Corporate Innovation Levels of Progression

Scoring profiles based on the Corporate Innovation Levels of Progression are provided in this manual to aid the team's scoring process. The teams should first consider the two dimensions (Process and Results) and review the Corporate Innovation Levels of Progression Scoring Profile sections. The scoring profiles will aid the team in further profiling and fine-tuning the percentile range in which the scores should fall.

Corporate Innovation Levels of Progression

1. **Launching (0-20%)**   The organization's leadership is beginning to understand the opportunities for promoting corporate innovation and entrepreneurial initiatives organization-wide. Leaders are in the beginning stages of promoting corporate innovation and entrepreneurial efforts, and in recognizing innovative and entrepreneurial practices. Leaders do not understand how innovation and entrepreneurial efforts can be aligned with the organization's strategic planning process.

2. **Evolving (20-40%)**   The organization is implementing corporate innovation and entrepreneurial efforts in some departments/ divisions corporate-wide. Senior leaders are beginning to support corporate-wide innovation and entrepreneurial initiatives and are recognizing some staff members and teams for their innovative and entrepreneurial practices. Senior staff and a few managers are reviewing the inclusion of a few corporate innovation and entrepreneurial initiatives within the organization's strategic planning process.

3. **Progressing (40-60%)**   The organization's senior leadership is committed to promoting and protecting corporate innovation and entrepreneurial efforts and has a well-defined plan to deploy its strategic efforts throughout the workforce. Customer/ vendor/ employee support systems are in place to ensure that ongoing corporate innovation and entrepreneurial recognition efforts are being initiated and managed throughout the organization. A separate Corporate Innovation Plan is being developed and aligned with the organization's strategic planning efforts.

4. **Accomplishing (60-80%)**   The organization's senior leaders promote on-going corporate innovation training and staff development offerings among their workforce, vendors and customer groups. A separate Corporate Innovation Plan has been developed and aligned with the organization's strategic plan. Managers, employees, vendors and customers are rewarded/ recognized for their involvement in promoting corporate innovation and entrepreneurial activities corporate-wide throughout the organization.

5. **Notable (80-100%)**   The organization's senior leadership is visibly involved in promoting corporate innovation and entrepreneurship efforts for their employees, vendors, customers, and communities in which the organization conducts business. The organization has become a community and industry model for its promotion of innovative thinking and has become a global benchmark in innovation for its training, employee leadership development, educational offerings, and staff recognition. The corporate innovation and entrepreneurial practices are well documented with results that have positive three- to five-year financial and market share trends within the organization.

Corporate Innovation Levels of Progression Scoring Profiles
1. Leadership

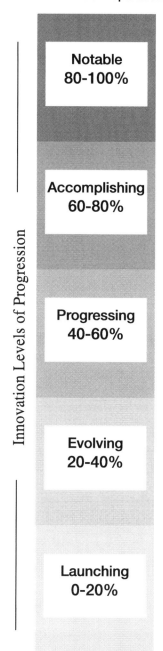

Notable 80-100%	• Senior leadership supports and promotes corporate innovation practices and formally rewards/recognizes all senior staff and managers who promote innovative initiatives throughout the workforce. • Senior leaders promote the organizations commitment to innovative practices in all industry, supplier/customer and public speeches. • Senior leadership promotes the organization's commitment to innovative practices in their Management Development Program and rewards Managers for promoting innovation among the workforce.
Accomplishing 60-80%	• Most senior leaders promote the organizations corporate innovation practices in their public speaking engagements. • Most senior leaders promote corporate innovation initiatives among employees, vendors and other key stakeholder groups. • Senior Leadership meets quarterly with employee teams, key vendors, partners, and customers regarding the use of innovative thinking to solve various corporate issues.
Progressing 40-60%	• Senior leaders are increasing their support of corporate innovation through their public speaking engagements with various industry and community groups. • Senior leadership share their corporate innovation values with employees, customers, partners, vendors, and outside organizations. • Senior Management is committed to public responsibility and community involvement regarding innovative corporate outreach opportunities.
Evolving 20-40%	• A few senior leaders and managers support corporate innovation among the workforce. • A few senior leaders and managers are beginning to support corporate innovation initiatives in their employee meetings and speaking engagements. • The organization's corporate policies and procedures reflect some commitment to corporate innovation.
Launching 0-20%	• Senior leadership and key managers do not support, nor promote corporate innovation. • Senior leadership is at the beginning stage of promoting corporate innovation as a competitive edge for the organization among various employee groups. • limited interest and concerns by senior staff in promoting innovative thinking among employees, and recognizing/rewarding employees who have identified innovative approaches to solving various corporate problems and/or issues.

Process Dimension (Categories 1-6)
Evaluation Factors

☑   **Approach** (methods used to accomplish the process)

☑   **Deployment** (application of the approach throughout the organization)

☑   **Learning** (refinement of the approach through cycles of evaluation)

☑   **Integration** (alignment of the approach throughout the organization)

Corporate Innovation Levels of Progression Scoring Profiles
2. Strategic Planning

World Class Preparation	
Notable 80-100%	• The strategic planning process includes highlighting innovative initiatives in the organizations short and longer-term planning process. • The organization seeks and receives input from employees, vendors, partners, and customers before developing its Corporate Innovation Plan that is being aligned with the organizations master strategic plan. • The strategic planning process is used to identify key corporate innovative initiatives that will help drive the organizations competitiveness in the marketplace.
Accomplishing 60-80%	• Senior management provides input and reviews all innovative projects that will help grow the organization's overall market opportunities to ensure that they are aligned with the organizations strategic goals and plans. • A Corporate Innovation Plan is linked to the organization's master strategic plan. • Managers are held accountable and rewarded for meeting short and longer-term strategic corporate innovation goals and objectives.
Progressing 40-60%	• Corporate innovation opportunities are considered when developing the organizations short and longer term planning. • Corporate innovation opportunities are being addressed in various cross-functional employee teams and their findings are being included in all the organizations short and longer-term strategic plans. • Employees at all levels are involved in the strategic planning process to help identify innovative strategic opportunities for the organization.
Evolving 20-40%	• A few corporate innovation opportunities are beginning to be identified and included in the organization's strategic planning considerations. • Some employees, vendors, partners, and customers are involved in identifying innovative strategic opportunities for the organization. • Some senior managers are beginning to consider the inclusion of innovative strategic opportunities in the organizations short and longer term strategic plans.
Launching 0-20%	• No employees, vendors, partners, or customers are involved in identifying innovative initiatives that could be incorporated into the organization's strategic planning process. • Corporate innovation has limited consideration during the organization's annual strategic planning process. • Senior leaders have no interest in corporate innovation being a strategic driver and being included in the organizations short and longer term strategic planning process.
Zero-Based Preparation	

Innovation Levels of Progression

Process Dimension (Categories 1-6)
Evaluation Factors

☑   **Approach** (methods used to accomplish the process)

☑   **Deployment** (application of the approach throughout the organization)

☑   **Learning** (refinement of the approach through cycles of evaluation)

☑   **Integration** (alignment of the approach throughout the organization)

Corporate Innovation Levels of Progression Scoring Profiles
3. Customer Focus

Innovation Levels of Progression	
World Class Preparation	
Notable **80-100%**	• The organization conducts surveys, focus groups, and exit interviews to determine customer requirements and concerns regarding corporate innovation. • The organization promotes trust and confidence in its products/ services and promotes employees use of innovative solutions to customer problems. • Corporate innovation is promoted among customer contact employees.
Accomplishing **60-80%**	• Effective feedback systems are in place to obtain critical customer and market feedback data on various innovative offerings. • Customer contact employees are given customer service relationship training using innovative problem-solving solutions. • Corporate innovation is promoted among customer contact employees to help solve customer problems.
Progressing **40-60%**	• Effective customer support is being put in place through innovative customer service initiatives. • A complaint management process that is promoting innovative resolutions to customer concerns is in place throughout the organization. • A formal recognition program is in place to recognize and reward all customer-contact employees who exhibit innovative solutions to resolve customer problems.
Evolving **20-40%**	• Some customer groups and markets are segmented to ensure that all their concerns are being addressed in an innovative and timely manner. • Customer follow-up system is being developed in several parts of the organization to address innovative service quality issues. • Innovative problem solving is being promoted among some customer service contact employees and a reward/recognition system is being planned to recognize their use of innovative solutions for customers.
Launching **0-20%**	• Organization is in the beginning stages of promoting trust and confidence among customers and applying innovative solutions. • Organization conducts limited surveys of its customers/markets regarding customer service issues/concerns and innovative resolutions. • Organization does not consider customers' complaints important enough to address in a timely manner with innovative resolutions.
Zero-Based Preparation	

Process Dimension (Categories 1-6)
Evaluation Factors

☑ **Approach** (methods used to accomplish the process)

☑ **Deployment** (application of the approach throughout the organization)

☑ **Learning** (refinement of the approach through cycles of evaluation)

☑ **Integration** (alignment of the approach throughout the organization)

Corporate Innovation Levels of Progression Scoring Profiles
4. Measurement, Analysis, and Knowledge Management

Innovation Levels of Progression	
World Class Preparation	
Notable 80-100%	• Processes and technology are in place to ensure safe, timely, accurate, valid, and useful innovation data/information are made available for employees, vendors, partners, and customers to access. • Competitive comparisons and benchmarking information and data are used to ensure that organizational knowledge and innovative solutions are kept current. • Data and information are analyzed organization-wide to translate into innovative corporate practices and resolutions.
Accomplishing 60-80%	• Employees have secure access to corporate innovation data throughout the organization. • Comparative data is collected, analyzed, and translated into useful information to ensure safety and security of the organizations intellectual capital and innovative practices. • Innovative processes and technologies are in place across the organization to ensure that corporate data is secure, updated, complete, timely, accurate, valid, and useful.
Progressing 40-60%	• Employees have secure access to corporate innovation data in many parts of the organization. • Most critical corporate innovation data is secure, complete, accurate, and timely. • Measures exist that gauge corporate innovation data/information effectiveness and security throughout the organization.
Evolving 20-40%	• Corporate innovation data exists for some key products/services and processes. • Organization is beginning to ensure that hardware and software that stores the organization's innovation data are reliable, secure, and user-friendly. • Corporate innovation data and knowledge that needs to be protected is being reviewed by senior leadership and various cross-functional employee teams.
Launching 0-20%	• Limited corporate innovation data is being protected and considered important to grow the organization's market share. • Collection of corporate innovation data is in the beginning stages within the organization and is being shared with some customers, vendors, and partners. • Senior leaders and managers have limited concern for overall protection of the organization's innovation data, intellectual capital, competitive practices, and best-practice knowledge.
Zero-Based Preparation	

Process Dimension (Categories 1-6)
Evaluation Factors

☑ **Approach** (methods used to accomplish the process)

☑ **Deployment** (application of the approach throughout the organization)

☑ **Learning** (refinement of the approach through cycles of evaluation)

☑ **Integration** (alignment of the approach throughout the organization)

Corporate Innovation Levels of Progression Scoring Profiles
5. Workforce Focus

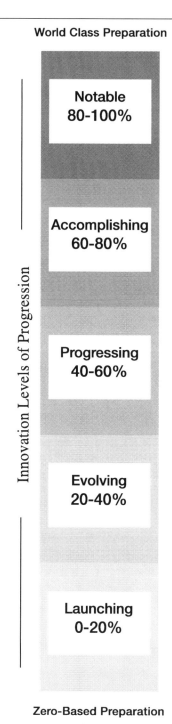

World Class Preparation

Notable
80-100%

Accomplishing
60-80%

Progressing
40-60%

Evolving
20-40%

Launching
0-20%

Zero-Based Preparation

Innovation Levels of Progression

	• Leadership promotes innovation through the organization's high performance work environment and through their employee recognition and reward system for submission of innovative ideas. • Organizational culture is characterized by innovation, open communication, high performance, and an engaged workforce. • Organization innovates its educational programs and services and its work processes by involving the workforce in producing innovative solutions for customers, and stakeholders.
	• Senior and middle management support and recognize employee involvement, and teamwork in producing high performance work, and taking intelligent risks to achieve innovation. • Employee idea sharing and innovation is encouraged and rewarded throughout the workforce. • Employees are empowered and rewarded when they identify process improvement issues through innovation.
	• Organization is beginning to incorporate cycle time, productivity and other efficiency and effectiveness factors into their innovative work processes. • Organization partners with suppliers to meet operational needs and enhance performance requirements of customers through innovation. • Management supports cross-functional teams' use of innovation to address workplace safety issues, accident prevention, inspection, root-cause analysis of failures, and recovery initiatives.
	• Managers in some parts of the organization support employee innovation in reviewing cycle time, productivity and other efficiency factors that impact work process throughout the organization. • Management is in the beginning stages of promoting a workforce management system that supports innovation, high performance and workforce engagement. • Employee training initiatives are beginning to promote innovation when addressing performance improvement issues.
	• Few employees within the organization are made aware of career progression within the workforce that promotes use of innovation for problem solving. • Workforce is seldom surveyed regarding their use of innovative solutions to customer problems. • Organization seldom addresses innovation, and "out of the box thinking" with the workforce.

Process Dimension (Categories 1-6)
Evaluation Factors

☑ **Approach** (methods used to accomplish the process)

☑ **Deployment** (application of the approach throughout the organization)

☑ **Learning** (refinement of the approach through cycles of evaluation)

☑ **Integration** (alignment of the approach throughout the organization)

Corporate Innovation Levels of Progression Scoring Profiles
6. Operations Focus

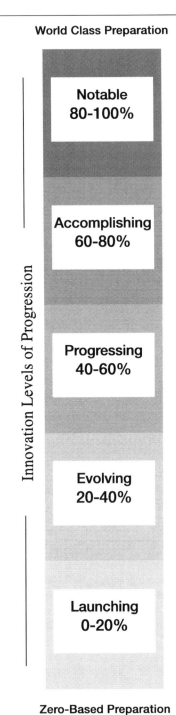

World Class Preparation

Notable
80-100%

Accomplishing
60-80%

Progressing
40-60%

Evolving
20-40%

Launching
0-20%

Zero-Based Preparation

Innovation Levels of Progression

Notable 80-100%	• Key innovative work processes/practices have been identified and documented throughout the organization. • Systematic approaches are used to document and to ensure that consistent innovative processes/practices are being followed throughout the workforce. • Key innovative processes are reviewed on an ongoing basis to reduce variability, and to ensure that key processes are current with the organization's present needs and future directions.
Accomplishing 60-80%	• Key innovative processes are documented, flowcharted, and controlled across most parts of the organization. • Comprehensive workforce climate assessments are conducted throughout the organization to gauge employees involvement and interest in innovative problem solving initiatives and resolutions. • Analytic problem-solving tools are used throughout the organization to improve key organizational processes and practices and to aid in producing innovative solutions/resolutions for various problem areas.
Progressing 40-60%	• Process assessments are conducted in several parts of the organization to ensure key innovative operational processes/practices have been identified, documented and flowcharted. • Customer, vendor, partner, and employee input are used periodically to flowchart and document key innovative processes/practices. • Organization has identified and documented several critical and key processes/practices which support corporate innovation.
Evolving 20-40%	• Corporate innovation is being promoted by a few senior leaders and managers to improve overall operational efficiency and productivity. • Some corporate processes/practices have been identified as needing to be more innovative and employee teams have been assigned to review. • Senior leadership has begun to promote innovative thinking as part of the evolving corporate culture to help ensure organizational sustainability in the market place.
Launching 0-20%	• Organization is in the beginning stages of promoting corporate innovation among the workforce. • A few key/critical processes/practices are identified and reviewed to improve workforce efficiency and consistency through the use of innovative thinking and problem solving. • Corporate innovation is promoted in limited areas of the organization.

Process Dimension (Categories 1-6)
Evaluation Factors

☑   **Approach** (methods used to accomplish the process)

☑   **Deployment** (application of the approach throughout the organization)

☑   **Learning** (refinement of the approach through cycles of evaluation)

☑   **Integration** (alignment of the approach throughout the organization)

Corporate Innovation Levels of Progression Scoring Profiles
7. Business Results

Innovation Levels of Progression	
World Class Preparation	
Notable 80-100%	• Customer satisfaction results regarding corporate innovative initiatives have shown positive results over the past three years. • Corporate innovation performance results have experienced a steady improvement over the past four years. • Employee suggestions for corporate sustainability improvements and innovative sustainable work practices show positive trends over the past three years.
Accomplishing 60-80%	• The organization's customer satisfaction results have shown several positive trends over the past three years based on corporate innovation initiatives that have improved cycle time and operational performance. • Key corporate innovation measures of the organization's budgetary, financial, and market results have improved over the past three years in several parts of the organization. • Comparative benchmark results reveal that the organization is emerging as an industry leader in its innovative delivery of training and employee development offerings.
Progressing 40-60%	• Key measures of innovative process effectiveness and efficiency within Operations, Shipping and Customer Contact reflects a two-year trend of positive results. • Vendor audit data for innovative externally provided programs, services and processes are showing improved outcomes. • Customer satisfaction with the organization's innovative practices reflects positive results over the past two years.
Evolving 20-40%	• Customer satisfaction with the organization's innovative practices shows some positive results and trends. • Some employee involvement in innovative problem solving teams has shown a few positive results over the past two years. • Employee climate survey results shows some positive trends over the past two years based on the organization's innovative practices.
Launching 0-20%	• Limited to no benchmark results are collected by the organization and used for comparative analysis and innovative practices. • Employee satisfaction data that addresses workforce issues are shared to identify major employee concerns, and to improve overall workforce practices and/or procedures through innovation. • The organization is beginning to use data to identify key customer issues that are important to maintaining competeveness through innovation.
Zero-Based Preparation	

Results Dimension (Category 7)
Evaluation Factors

☑ **Performance Levels** (position of data performance)

☑ **Trends** (rate and breadth of data)

☑ **Comparisons** (results relative to appropriate benchmarks)

☑ **Linkage** (alignment of data with key organizational initiatives)

☑ **Gap** (missing segments of data)

2 How to Use the Manual

How to Use the Corporate Innovation Assessment Manual

This manual is designed to serve as an easy-to-use guide for an organization's cross-functional self-assessment team(s) to assess and score its corporate innovation efforts.

This manual can be used to provide a due diligence for an organization's corporate innovation efforts and to provide a template for its self-assessment and strategic planning regarding corporate innovation initiatives. In addition, the manual provides guidance for employees and employee teams to score their departments or total organization in many areas and serves as an annual benchmark for corporate innovation improvement and a strategic guide for short-term and longer-term corporate innovation planning. The manual assists employees in determining their organization's innovation strategies and transformational readiness. The manual can also be used to help employees collect corporate data to benchmark against other "best practice" organizations and to ultimately develop a Corporate Innovation Plan.

How to Begin and Prepare for an Assessment

The assessment of an organization should begin with the full support and sponsorship of the organization's senior leadership. The senior leadership should appoint a corporate innovation assessment team administrator.

The first step in preparing for the assessment should include conducting a corporate innovation assessment briefing for senior leadership. This session can be conducted by the organization's Chief Innovation Officer (CIO) or the person who has been selected by senior leadership. The staff member appointed to conduct the briefing should review this manual and have a thorough understanding of corporate training and employee development issues before conducting the session.

In addition, senior leadership must be educated in strategic issues that relate to a corporate innovation to appreciate the value of conducting the assessment. Several activities are recommended to help senior leaders develop an understanding of corporate innovation issues. These include the following:

- Reading books and articles about corporate innovation (a suggested resource list is included in this manual after Appendix H)
- Benchmarking other public/private organizations to review best practices (see Appendix B)

After senior leaders have been briefed, the assessment team administrator should begin the process of soliciting assessment team members. Many organizations solicit members through their corporate newsletter, electronic mail, or a personal letter sent from the organizations President/CEO inviting participation. Team members' selections should be considered from a group of employees who have expressed an interest in better understanding corporate innovation issues to improve their organization's transformational infrastructure.

Once team members have been selected, it is recommended that an assessment workshop be conducted by the assessment team administrator or team participants who have an understanding of employee training and development delivery issues as they relate to a corporate innovation. The workshop may include using a case study for the team to practice identifying organizational strengths and opportunities for corporate innovation improvement in at least one or two categories. During the workshop, the team will discuss each category and determine "What does this mean for my organization?" The use of this manual will help the team translate corporate innovation findings and issues into simple language for their own organization-wide assessment.

Assessing the Organization

Team Member Selection

Assessment team members should represent a cross-section of employees. All departments throughout the parent organization should be represented on the teams. Diversity adds value and strength to each assessment team.

In larger organizations, seven corporate innovation assessment category sub-teams would need to be developed. A subject matter expert (SME) for a particular category should be elected as the category team leader. In smaller organizations where there are a limited number of personnel who could serve on assessment teams, all categories can be assessed by one team. Following are some sample assessment team compositions:

ASSESSMENT TEAM COMPOSITION (LARGE ORGANIZATION)
(20 to 50 MEMBERS)

Team 1: Leadership

CEO, President, or Senior VP (Team Leader)
Chief Innovation Officer (CIO)
Director of Legal
Director of Public Policy
Manager of Operations
Director of Marketing
Vendor
Partner

Team 2: Strategic Planning

VP, Strategic Planning (Team Leader)
Chief Innovation Officer (CIO)
Director
Manager
Supervisor
Director of Marketing
Vendor
Partner

Team 3: Customer Focus

VP, Marketing (Team Leader)
Director
Manager
Supervisor
Customer Service Manager
Vendor
Partner

Team 4: Measurement, Analysis and Knowledge Management

VP, IT (Team Leader)
Director of IT
Manager
Supervisor
Customer Service Manager
Vendor
Partner

Team 5: Workforce Focus

VP, Human Resources (Team Leader)
Director
Manager
Supervisor
Customer Service Manager
Vendor
Partner

Team 6: Process Management

VP, Operations (Team Leader)
Director
Manager
Supervisor
Customer Service Manager
Vendor
Partner

Team 7: Results

VP, Strategic Planning (Team Leader)
Director
Manager
Supervisor
Customer Service Manager
Vendor
Partner

Note: Some teams may decide to assess only selected categories within their organization that appear weak in deploying corporate innovation initiatives. This manual allows for complete flexibility regarding the extent to which an organization conducts its assessment.

ASSESSMENT TEAM COMPOSITION (SMALL ORGANIZATION)
(6 to 8 Members)
Team Assesses All Seven Corporate Innovation Categories

- President/CEO or Senior VP (Team Leader)
- Chief Innovation Officer (CIO)
- Director
- Manager
- Supervisor
- Customer Service Manager
- Vendor/Partner

Pre-Assessment Meeting for Each Team

Corporate Innovation Category team(s) will need to hold a pre-assessment planning meeting to identify individuals to be interviewed during the assessment. Dates and interview times need to be agreed upon during this session, and an agenda and timetable should be prepared. After the team selects the individuals within the organization to be interviewed, a team leader needs to contact all persons to be interviewed.

Coordination of Assessment Team Schedules

The assessment team administrator should coordinate all seven Category team schedules with Corporate Innovation Category team leaders and develop an overall assessment interview plan and timetable (see Appendix D). This schedule and timetable should then be submitted to the senior leadership of the organization for review and approval.

Team Interview of Selected Participants

After approval has been secured from senior leadership, each team is ready to begin its interview process with selected participants. The entire category team(s) will take turns interviewing the participants. This allows for more interaction and input for the assessment team. During the interview process, all assessment team members will have a copy for this manual in hand and will make notes under each of the questions. Each category team may choose to interview two to three groups of participants representing various levels throughout the organization. Interviewing hints and tips are provided in Appendix D. A corporate innovation documentation list form is provided in Appendix E for the team(s) to use to list documents used to validate participant responses to the interview questions.

Assessment Team Consensus and Scoring of the Category

After all category interviews have been completed, the category team leaders will hold a consensus review meeting in which all team members will review the findings regarding areas identified as strengths and opportunities for improvement. The team will reach a consensus and assign each item a percentile score and will ultimately award the category a total point score. A quick and easy organizational assessment for the organization's vendors, partners, and customers is provided (see Appendix A) to help determine to what extent vendor and customer organizations have approached and deployed corporate sustainability initiatives within their own organizations. This quick assessment may also be used as a preliminary analysis of one's own organization or to benchmark another organization's corporate innovation progress.

Entire Assessment Report Consolidated and Delivered

All seven Corporate Innovation Category teams will deliver their assessment to the assessment team administrator. The assessment team administrator will meet with all category team leaders to review results. After the assessment team administrator and all seven category team leaders have reached a consensus on the strengths, opportunities for improvement, corporate innovation planning issues, category percentile scores, and the overall assessment point score, the assessment is finalized and a Corporate Innovation Plan can be developed (see Chapter 10). The completed assessment and Corporate Innovation Plan is then delivered to the President/CEO and the other senior staff members of the organization. The entire assessment process can take as little as two weeks or as much as one month to complete.

Organizational Overview
(Complete before conducting Corporate Innovation assessment)

Corporate Innovation Assessment Period Review dates: _____ to _____

1.0 Organizational Policies and Procedures

1.1 Does your organization have published vision, mission, and values statements?
Yes ☐   No ☐

1.2 Does your organization have a published Organization Chart?
Yes ☐   No ☐

1.3 Does your organization have a formal Strategic Plan?
Yes ☐   No ☐

2.0 Project Improvement Teams for Corporate Innovation Planning

2.1 Total employee population:

2.2 Project Teams

Name of Project Team	Employee Projects			Functional Area Team (Check Area)							
	Hours	Number of Participants	Date of Project Completion	Sales & Marketing	Human Resources	Program/ Course Development	Finance/ Accounting	Administration	Shipping/ Receiving	Other	

3.0 Customers/ Vendors/ Partners

3.1 List key customers   Number of key customers _____

Key Customer Names	Date Customer Relationship Began	Length of Time as a Customer	Unique Innovation Requirements

3.2 List key vendors/partners   Number of key vendors/partners _____

Key vendor/Partner Names	Date Partnership Began	Length of Time as a vendor/Partner	Unique innovation Requirements

4.0 Corporate Innovation Activities

List other activities that may have been carried out in your organization during this assessment review period.

Activity	Objective

5.0 Corporate Innovation Training/Development

5.1 Does your organization have a training budget for employee training and development?
Yes ☐   No ☐

5.2 What was your annual training expenditure(s) for employee training/development activities during this assessment review period?

5.3 Provide a list of employee training/development activities conducted during this assessment review period.

Internal and External Courses and Workshops	Hours	Number of Participants	Date of Training	Functional Area Team (Check Area)							
				Sales & Marketing	Human Resources	Program/ Course Design	Finance/ Accounting	Manager/ Supervisor	Shipping/ Receiving	Other	

6.0 Corporate Innovation Assessments

6.1 Does your organization conduct assessments on Corporate Innovation?
Yes ☐   No ☐

If yes, please specify the areas and frequency of the assessment(s) being conducted during this review period.

Areas	Frequency
Internal Assessments	
External Assessments	
Others	

7.0 Trends/ Improvements for the Organization's Corporate Innovation Plan

7.1 Are trends of key Corporate Innovation offerings and initiatives being tracked regularly?
Yes ☐   No ☐
(If yes, list and collect documents.)

Documents	How often tracked?

7.2 What are your organizational challenges for Corporate Innovation?

Organizational Challenges

Competitive Environment

Strategic Challenges

Performance Challenges

NOTES

Seven Steps for Successful Assessment Implementation and Manual Use

The following seven steps will further explain how this manual will be useful in simplifying the assessment process for the organization.

Step One   Complete the Organizational Overview

The assessment team administrator and senior staff should complete the organizational overview before the team(s) conduct the corporate innovation assessment. The organizational overview is the most appropriate starting point for the assessment and will provide a snapshot of the organization's corporate innovation initiatives before the team(s) begin the assessment process. The information collected in the organizational overview should be used to identify potential issues and challenges. In addition, it may be used for an initial self-assessment.

Step Two   Review Questions

Following the description of the category are corporate innovation questions that have been simplified so they are more understandable and user-friendly. This allows a clearer and more precise corporate innovation assessment to be conducted.

The questions should be posed to different levels of employees throughout the organization. The assessment team should divide this task among its members.

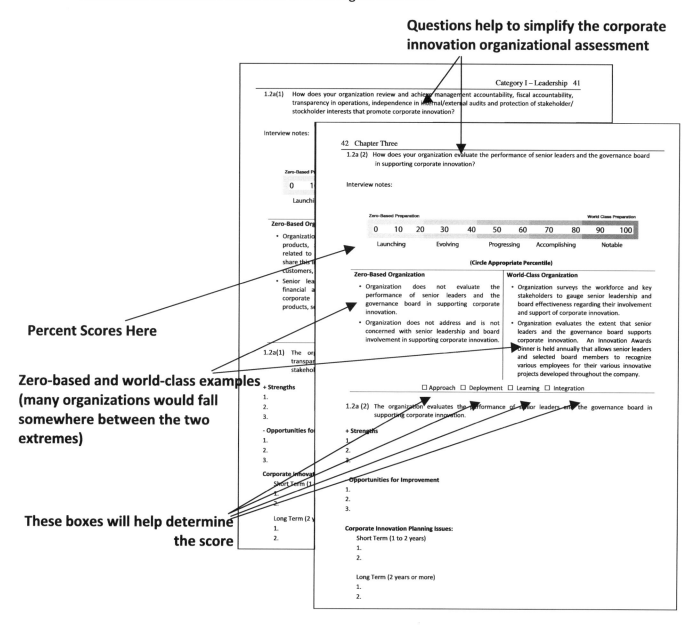

Questions help to simplify the corporate innovation organizational assessment

Percent Scores Here

Zero-based and world-class examples (many organizations would fall somewhere between the two extremes)

These boxes will help determine the score

Step Three   Review Zero-Based and World-Class Examples

Before recording answers to the questions, review the examples of zero-based and world-class organizations' corporate innovation initiatives that appear in the center of the page.

Below the examples appear four boxes labeled Approach, Deployment, Learning, and Integration. These boxes will aid in assessing the kinds of information and/or data the organization has in place and will aid the team in scoring the question (Refer to page 5).

Step Four   Make Interview Notes

Near the top of the page under each question is an interview notes section for recording answers to the questions given by employees as they are being interviewed by the assessment team. This data should be used to determine strengths, opportunities, and corporate innovation strategic planning issues located in the lower portion of the page.

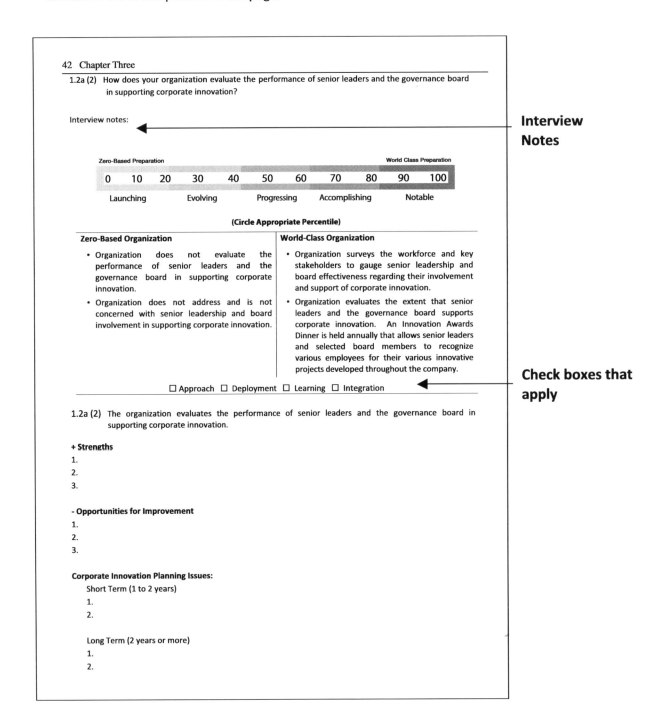

Step Five   List Comments for Strengths and Improvement

On the lower half of the page, the question is restated. After the interviews are completed, review the interview notes. The team will then list strengths and opportunities for improvement. All comments should be written in short, complete sentences.

42   Chapter Three

1.2a (2) How does your organization evaluate the performance of senior leaders and the governance board in supporting corporate innovation?

Interview notes:

Zero-Based Preparation								World Class Preparation		
0	10	20	30	40	50	60	70	80	90	100
Launching		Evolving			Progressing		Accomplishing		Notable	

(Circle Appropriate Percentile)

Zero-Based Organization	World-Class Organization
• Organization does not evaluate the performance of senior leaders and the governance board in supporting corporate innovation.	• Organization surveys the workforce and key stakeholders to gauge senior leadership and board effectiveness regarding their involvement and support of corporate innovation.
• Organization does not address and is not concerned with senior leadership and board involvement in supporting corporate innovation.	• Organization evaluates the extent that senior leaders and the governance board supports corporate innovation. An Innovation Awards Dinner is held annually that allows senior leaders and selected board members to recognize various employees for their various innovative projects developed throughout the company.

☐ Approach ☐ Deployment ☐ Learning ☐ Integration

1.2a (2) The organization evaluates the performance of senior leaders and the governance board in supporting corporate innovation.

+ Strengths
1.
2.
3.

- Opportunities for Improvement
1.
2.
3.

Corporate Innovation Planning Issues:
    Short Term (1 to 2 years)
    1.
    2.

    Long Term (2 years or more)
    1.
    2.

Question is restated

Step Six   List Corporate Innovation Strategic Planning Issues

After reviewing the interview notes, strengths, and opportunities for improvement, the assessment team should list any corporate innovation planning issues. These planning issues are divided into Short Term (1 to 2 years) and Long Term (2 years or more).

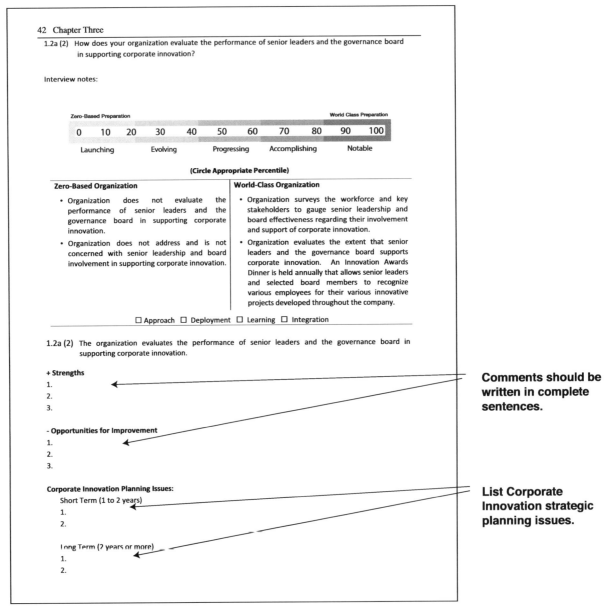

Step Seven   Score Assessment Items

The assessment is broken down into seven categories:

1. Leadership

2. Strategic Planning

3. Customer Focus

4. Measurement, Analysis, and Knowledge Management

5. Workforce Focus

6. Process Management

7. Results

These seven categories are divided into 18 assessment items; i.e., 1.1, 1.2, 2.1, 2.2, and the 18 assessment items are broken down into 89 areas; i.e., 1.1a(1), 1.1b). The percent score is reflective of the strengths and opportunities for improvement of the areas within each assessment item. Thus, throughout the assessment, all 18 items will obtain a percent score. All assessment item percent scores will be transferred to the **Corporate Innovation Score Sheet** located at the end of Chapter 9. A graph illustrating the **hierarchy of corporate Innovation assessment needs** visually presents the percent scores of each assessment category. This graph follows the Corporate Innovation Score Sheet at the end of Chapter 9.

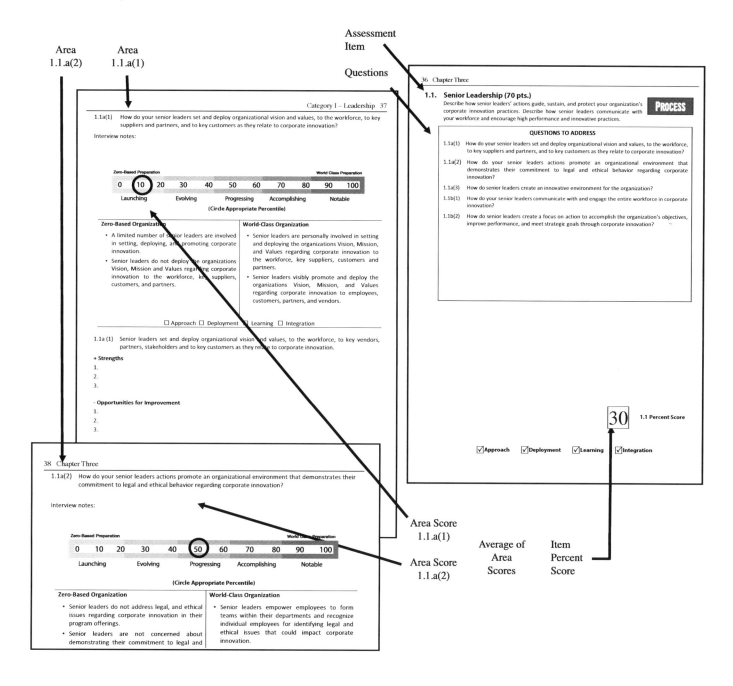

The assessment scores will ultimately be reviewed, prioritized, and transformed into actionable strategies for corporate innovation improvement, and a corporate innovation plan can be developed. The transformation process for consolidating corporate innovation assessment findings into a corporate innovation plan is explained in detail in Chapter 10 of the manual.

NOTES

NOTES

3

Category 1
Leadership

1 Leadership (120 pts.) [24]

The *Leadership* category examines how senior leaders' personal actions guide corporate innovation. It also asks about your organization's governance system and how your organization fulfills its legal, ethical, and societal responsibilities and supports its key communities.

1.1.   Senior Leadership (70 pts.)

Describe how senior leaders' actions guide, sustain, and protect your organization's corporate innovation practices. Describe how senior leaders communicate with your workforce and encourage high performance and innovative practices.

QUESTIONS TO ADDRESS

1.1a(1)   How do your senior leaders set and deploy organizational vision and values, to the workforce, to key suppliers and partners, and to key customers as they relate to corporate innovation?

1.1a(2)   How do your senior leaders actions promote an organizational environment that demonstrates their commitment to legal and ethical behavior regarding corporate innovation?

1.1a(3)   How do senior leaders create an innovative environment for the organization?

1.1b(1)   How do your senior leaders communicate with and engage the entire workforce in corporate innovation?

1.1b(2)   How do senior leaders create a focus on action to accomplish the organization's objectives, improve performance, and meet strategic goals through corporate innovation?

1.1 Percent Score

☑ Approach   ☑ Deployment   ☑ Learning   ☑ Integration

1.1a(1)   How do your senior leaders set and deploy organizational vision and values, to the workforce, to key suppliers and partners, and to key customers as they relate to corporate innovation?

Interview notes:

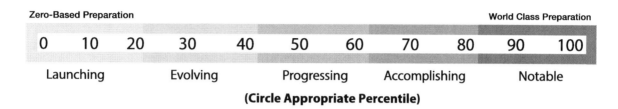

Zero-Based Preparation									World Class Preparation	
0	10	20	30	40	50	60	70	80	90	100
Launching		Evolving			Progressing		Accomplishing		Notable	

(Circle Appropriate Percentile)

Zero-Based Organization	**World-Class Organization**
• A limited number of senior leaders are involved in setting, deploying, and promoting corporate innovation. • Senior leaders do not deploy the organizations Vision, Mission and Values regarding corporate innovation to the workforce, key suppliers, customers, and partners.	• Senior leaders are personally involved in setting and deploying the organizations Vision, Mission, and Values regarding corporate innovation to the workforce, key suppliers, customers and partners. • Senior leaders visibly promote and deploy the organizations Vision, Mission, and Values regarding corporate innovation to employees, customers, partners, and vendors.

☐ Approach ☐ Deployment ☐ Learning ☐ Integration

1.1a (1)   Senior leaders set and deploy organizational vision and values, to the workforce, to key vendors, partners, stakeholders and to key customers as they relate to corporate innovation.

+ Strengths

1.

2.

3.

- Opportunities for Improvement

1.

2.

3.

Corporate Innovation Planning Issues:

Short Term (1 to 2 years)

1.

2.

Long Term (2 years or more)

1.

2.

1.1a(2)   How do your senior leaders actions promote an organizational environment that demonstrates their commitment to legal and ethical behavior regarding corporate innovation?

Interview notes:

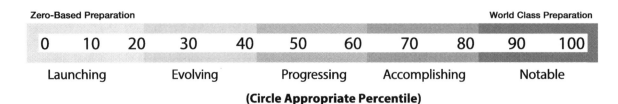

(Circle Appropriate Percentile)

Zero-Based Organization	**World-Class Organization**
• Senior leaders do not address legal, and ethical issues regarding corporate innovation in their program offerings. • Senior leaders are not concerned about demonstrating their commitment to legal and ethical behavior regarding corporate innovation.	• Senior leaders empower employees to form teams within their departments and recognize individual employees for identifying legal and ethical issues that could impact corporate innovation. • Senior leaders have formed "study groups" throughout the organization so that concerned employees identify and address legal and ethical issues related to corporate innovation.

☐ Approach   ☐ Deployment   ☐ Learning   ☐ Integration

1.1a (2)   Senior leaders actions promote an organizational environment that demonstrates their commitment to legal and ethical behavior regarding corporate innovation.

+ Strengths

1.

2.

3.

- Opportunities for Improvement

1.

2.

3.

Corporate Innovation Planning Issues:

    Short Term (1 to 2 Years)

    1.

    2.

    Long Term (2 Years of more)

    1.

    2.

1.1a(3)   How do senior leaders create an innovative environment for the organization?

Interview notes:

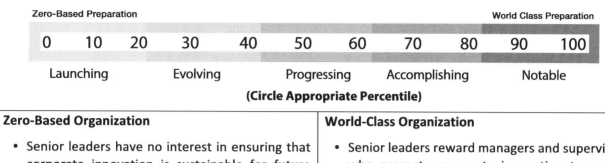

(Circle Appropriate Percentile)

Zero-Based Organization	World-Class Organization
• Senior leaders have no interest in ensuring that corporate innovation is sustainable for future generations of employees, customers, and vendors. • Senior leaders do not associate the identification of corporate innovation opportunities as a longer-term strategy for organizational sustainability.	• Senior leaders reward managers and supervisors who promote corporate innovation to ensure future growth and development of personnel throughout the organization. • Organization conducts annual corporate innovation surveys to gauge senior leaders involvement in innovative practices throughout the company.

☐ Approach ☐ Deployment ☐ Learning ☐ Integration

1.1a (3) Senior leaders create an innovative environment for the organization.

+ Strengths

1.

2.

3.

- Opportunities for Improvement

1.

2.

3.

Corporate Innovation Planning Issues:

Short Term (1 to 2 years)

1.

2.

Long Term (2 years or more)

1.

2.

1.1b(1)   How do your senior leaders communicate with and engage the entire workforce in corporate innovation?

Interview notes:

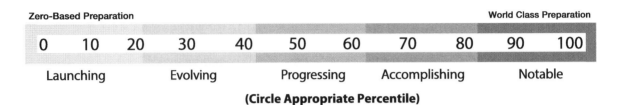

Launching   Evolving   Progressing   Accomplishing   Notable

(Circle Appropriate Percentile)

Zero-Based Organization	World-Class Organization
• Senior leaders do not review and assess innovative opportunities as they relate to educational and leadership readiness and capabilities for employees and management staff. • Senior leaders rarely review and assess innovative initiatives that are being developed and promoted throughout the workforce.	• Senior leaders hold all employees accountable for reviewing and identifying innovative development opportunities within their work areas. Senior staff meet annually with employees to reward and recognize their efforts in participating and promoting corporate innovation efforts. • Senior leaders review corporate innovation initiatives on a semi-annual basis and use their findings to ensure that innovative practices are being promoted and followed throughout the company.

☐ Approach   ☐ Deployment   ☐ Learning   ☐ Integration

1.1b (1)   Senior leaders communicate with and engage the entire workforce in corporate innovation.

+ Strengths

1.

2.

3.

- Opportunities for Improvement

1.

2.

3.

Corporate Innovation Planning Issues:

Short Term (1 to 2 years)

1.

2.

Long Term (2 years or more)

1.

2.

1.1b(2)   How do senior leaders create a focus on action to accomplish the organizations objectives, improve performance, and meet strategic goals through corporate innovation?

Interview notes:

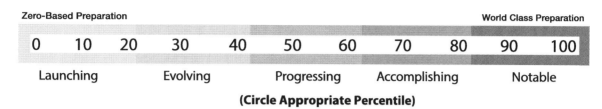

| Zero-Based Preparation | | | | | | | | | World Class Preparation |
| 0 | 10 | 20 | 30 | 40 | 50 | 60 | 70 | 80 | 90 | 100 |

Launching   Evolving   Progressing   Accomplishing   Notable

(Circle Appropriate Percentile)

Zero-Based Organization	World-Class Organization
• Senior leaders have not identified performance measures to gauge the effectiveness of key innovative workforce practices. • Senior leaders have identified limited key corporate performance measures to gauge the effectiveness of various innovative workforce practices, and only random reviews of the data are made and used by senior staff to gauge the organization's overall performance.	• Senior leaders review on a monthly basis technological and organizational improvement innovations that are being conducted by the Corporate Innovation for workforce and leadership development. • Senior leaders promote innovative performance improvement practices through the use of Six Sigma and Root Cause Analysis (RCA) to identify key workforce performance issues that need to be addressed.

☐ Approach   ☐ Deployment   ☐ Learning   ☐ Integration

1.1b(2)   Senior leaders create a focus on action to accomplish the organizations objectives, improve performance, and meet strategic goals through corporate innovation.

+ Strengths
1.
2.
3.

- Opportunities for Improvement
1.
2.
3.

Corporate Innovation Planning Issues:
    Short Term (1 to 2 years)
    1.
    2.

    Long Term (2 years or more)
    1.
    2.

1.2.   Governance and Societal Responsibilities (50 pts.)

Describe your organization's governance system and approach to leadership improvement in maintaining corporate innovation. Describe how your organization assures legal and ethical behavior, fulfills its societal responsibilities, and supports its key communities through corporate innovation.

QUESTIONS TO ADDRESS

1.2a(1)   How does your organization review and achieve management accountability, fiscal accountability, transparency in operations, independence in internal/external audits and protection of stakeholder/ stockholder interests that promote corporate innovation?

1.2a (2)   How does your organization evaluate the performance of senior leaders and the governance board in supporting corporate innovation?

1.2b (1)   How does your organization anticipate, address, and prepare any adverse impacts on society of your innovative services, products and operations?

1.2c (1)   How does your organization consider societal well-being and benefits as part of your strategy and daily operations through corporate innovation?

1.2c (2)   How does your organization actively support and strengthen key communities in which business is conducted through corporate innovation?

1.2 Percent Score

☑Approach   ☑Deployment   ☑Learning   ☑Integration

1.2a(1)   How does your organization review and achieve management accountability, fiscal accountability, transparency in operations, independence in internal/external audits and protection of stakeholder/ stockholder interests that promote corporate innovation?

Interview notes:

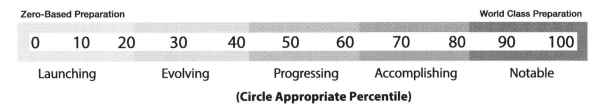

(Circle Appropriate Percentile)

Zero-Based Organization	World-Class Organization
• Organization does not address fiscal issues of its products, services, and operations that are related to corporate innovation and does not share this information with employees, vendors, customers, partners, and stakeholders.	• Organization developed a brochure outlining key financial and operational issues related to innovative practices that impact fiscal accountability, audits, and transparency issues related to operations, trademarks, patents, and distributes the brochure to key vendors, partners, customers, and stakeholders.
• Senior leadership is not concerned about financial and operational issues related to corporate innovation that enhances its products, services, and operations.	• Senior leaders hold public forums with communities where business is conducted to address operational concerns related to the company's innovative practices.

☐ Approach   ☐ Deployment   ☐ Learning   ☐ Integration

1.2a(1)   The organization reviews and achieves management accountability, fiscal accountability, transparency in operations, independence in internal/external audits and protection of stakeholder/stockholder interests that promote corporate innovation.

+ Strengths

1.

2.

3.

- Opportunities for Improvement

1.

2.

3.

Corporate Innovation Planning Issues:

Short Term (1 to 2 years)

1.

2.

Long Term (2 years or more)

1.

2.

1.2a (2)   How does your organization evaluate the performance of senior leaders and the governance board in supporting corporate innovation?

Interview notes:

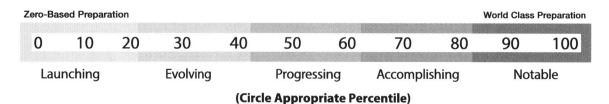

Zero-Based Preparation   World Class Preparation

| 0 | 10 | 20 | 30 | 40 | 50 | 60 | 70 | 80 | 90 | 100 |

Launching   Evolving   Progressing   Accomplishing   Notable

(Circle Appropriate Percentile)

Zero-Based Organization	World-Class Organization
• Organization does not evaluate the performance of senior leaders and the governance board in supporting corporate innovation.	• Organization surveys the workforce and key stakeholders to gauge senior leadership and board effectiveness regarding their involvement and support of corporate innovation.
• Organization does not address and is not concerned with senior leadership and board involvement in supporting corporate innovation.	• Organization evaluates the extent that senior leaders and the governance board supports corporate innovation. An Innovation Awards Dinner is held annually that allows senior leaders and selected board members to recognize various employees for their various innovative projects developed throughout the company.

☐ Approach ☐ Deployment ☐ Learning ☐ Integration

1.2a (2)   The organization evaluates the performance of senior leaders and the governance board in supporting corporate innovation.

+ Strengths

1.

2.

3.

- Opportunities for Improvement

1.

2.

3.

Corporate Innovation Planning Issues:

Short Term (1 to 2 years)

1.

2.

Long Term (2 years or more)

1.

2.

1.2b (1)   How does your organization anticipate, address, and prepare any adverse impacts on society of your innovative services, products and operations?

Interview notes:

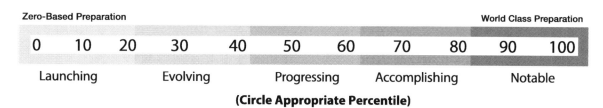

Zero-Based Preparation   World Class Preparation

| 0 | 10 | 20 | 30 | 40 | 50 | 60 | 70 | 80 | 90 | 100 |

Launching   Evolving   Progressing   Accomplishing   Notable

(Circle Appropriate Percentile)

Zero-Based Organization	World-Class Organization
• Organization does not have a Corporate Innovation Plan in place that addresses adverse societal impacts of their products, services, and operations. • Organization has no formal processes in place to safeguard innovative corporate practices and to anticipate, address and prepare for any adverse impacts on services, products and operations.	• Organization has developed a code of ethical conduct regarding innovative corporate practices that addresses any adverse societal impacts on services, products and operations. This statement is distributed to all employees, vendors, partners and customers. • Organization has developed a protocol, that addresses possible adverse societal impacts of its innovative services, products and operations that could affect future stakeholder transactions and interactions.

☐ Approach   ☐ Deployment   ☐ Learning   ☐ Integration

1.2b (1)   The organization anticipates, addresses, and prepares any adverse impacts on society of innovative services, products and operations.

+ Strengths

1.
2.
3.

- Opportunities for Improvement

1.
2.
3.

Corporate Innovation Planning Issues:

Short Term (1 to 2 years)

1.
2.

Long Term (2 years or more)

1.
2.

1.2c (1)   How does your organization consider societal well-being and benefits as part of your strategy and daily operations through corporate innovation?

Interview notes:

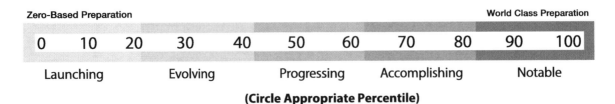

(Circle Appropriate Percentile)

Zero-Based Organization	World-Class Organization
• Organization does not consider innovative societal well-being and benefit planning issues as part of their corporate strategy and daily operations. • Organization does not have a process in place to address innovative societal well-being and benefit efforts among employees, vendors, customers, stakeholders, and community groups.	• Organization has identified innovative key short and longer-term societal well-being goals, known as the "triple Bottom-Line" (Economic-Environmental-Social), in their long term Strategic Plan and reward employees who meet and/or exceed these corporate goals within their daily operations. • Organization formally promotes innovative societal well-being practices and benefits in their strategic plan and daily operations.

☐ Approach   ☐ Deployment   ☐ Learning   ☐ Integration

1.2c (1)   The organization considers societal well-being and benefits as part of the strategy and daily operations through corporate innovation.

+ Strengths

1.
2.
3.

- Opportunities for Improvement

1.
2.
3.

Corporate Innovation Planning Issues:

Short Term (1 to 2 years)

1.
2.

Long Term (2 years or more)

1.
2.

1.2c(2)   How does your organization actively support and strengthen key communities in which business is conducted through corporate innovation?

Interview notes:

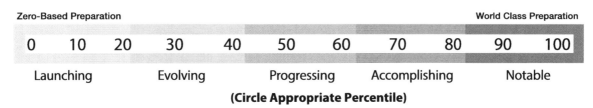

(Circle Appropriate Percentile)

Zero-Based Organization	**World-Class Organization**
• Organization does not promote corporate innovation within the communities in which business is conducted and has little concern for providing any community support. • Organization does not promote innovative practices within communities in which business is conducted.	• Organization recognizes and rewards employees who promote corporate innovation within programs that support the communities in which the company's business outreach extends. • Organization provides extra pay incentives to employees who volunteer their time to promote and are involved in innovative practices/ programs that help communities in which the company's business outreach is extended.

☐ Approach ☐ Deployment ☐ Learning ☐ Integration

1.2c(2)   The organization actively supports and strengthens key communities in which business is conducted through corporate innovation.

+ Strengths

1.
2.
3.

- Opportunities for Improvement

1.
2.
3.

Corporate Innovation Planning Issues:

Short Term (1 to 2 years)
1.
2.

Long Term (2 years or more)
1.
2.

NOTES

4 Category 2 Strategic Planning

2 Strategic Planning (85 pts.) [25]

The Strategic Planning category examines how your organization develops strategic objectives and action plans for corporate innovation. Also examined are how your chosen strategic objectives and action plans are deployed and changed if circumstances require, and how progress is measured.

2.1   Strategy Development (40 pts.)

Describe how your organization establishes its corporate innovation strategy to address its overall strategic challenges and leverage its strategic advantages. Summarize your organization's key strategic objectives and their related goals.

QUESTIONS TO ADDRESS

2.1a (1)   How does your organization conduct strategic planning for corporate innovation?

2.1a(2)   How does your organization ensure that strategic planning addresses key corporate innovation factors (i.e., customer/market needs, competitive environment, technology needs, human resources, redirecting resources, environmental issues, financial risks, societal risks, national/global economy changes, partner/supply chain needs, and human rights)?

2.1b (1)   What are your organization's key strategic objectives for corporate innovation and your timetable for accomplishing them?

2.1b (2)   How does your organization address your strategic challenges and advantages for corporate innovation?

2.1 Percent Score

☑Approach   ☑Deployment   ☑Learning   ☑Integration

2.1a (1)   How does your organization conduct strategic planning for corporate innovation?

Interview notes:

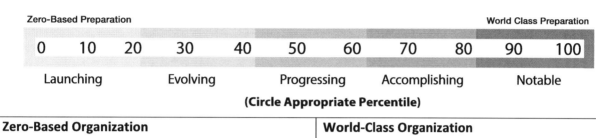

Zero-Based Preparation									World Class Preparation	
0	10	20	30	40	50	60	70	80	90	100
Launching		Evolving			Progressing		Accomplishing		Notable	

(Circle Appropriate Percentile)

Zero-Based Organization	**World-Class Organization**
• Organization does not have an overall strategic planning process in place for corporate innovation. • Organization has not developed a vision and identified strategic objectives to implement a plan for corporate innovation.	• Organization has each division identify and develop short and longer-term objectives for corporate innovation. All division plans are merged into an organization-wide plan. • Organization involves input from all employee levels when developing an overall strategic planning process for corporate innovation.

☐ Approach   ☐ Deployment   ☐ Learning   ☐ Integration

2.1a (1)   The organization conducts strategic planning for corporate innovation.

+ Strengths

1.

2.

3.

- Opportunities for Improvement

1.

2.

3.

Corporate Innovation Planning Issues:

Short Term (1 to 2 years)

1.

2.

Long Term (2 years or more)

1.

2.

2.1a(2)   How does your organization ensure that strategic planning addresses key corporate innovation factors (i.e., customer/market needs, competitive environment, technology needs, human resources, redirecting resources, environmental issues, financial risks, societal risks, national/global economy changes, partner/supply chain needs, and human rights)?

Interview notes:

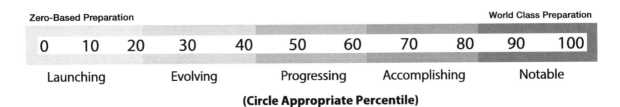

(Circle Appropriate Percentile)

Zero-Based Organization	**World-Class Organization**
• Organization has not considered key corporate innovation factors in its strategic plan such as corporate governance, risk and crisis management, environmental performance (eco-efficiency), human capital development, and labor practices. • Organization has not identified key corporate innovation factors to develop a planning approach that will protect the organizations competitive knowledge, intellectual assets, trademarks and patents.	• Organization has a strategic plan to manage corporate innovation issues and to mitigate future risks for the organizations management of the enterprise. • Organization's strategic plan for corporate innovation addresses competitive knowledge, intellectual assets, trademark and patent protections.

☐ Approach ☐ Deployment ☐ Learning ☐ Integration

2.1a (2)   The organization addresses key corporate innovation factors in its strategic plan.

+ Strengths

1.
2.
3.

- Opportunities for Improvement

1.
2.
3.

Corporate Innovation Planning Issues:

Short Term (1 to 2 years)

1.
2.

Long Term (2 years or more)

1.
2.

2.1b (1)   What are your organization's key strategic objectives for corporate innovation and your timetable for accomplishing them?

Interview notes:

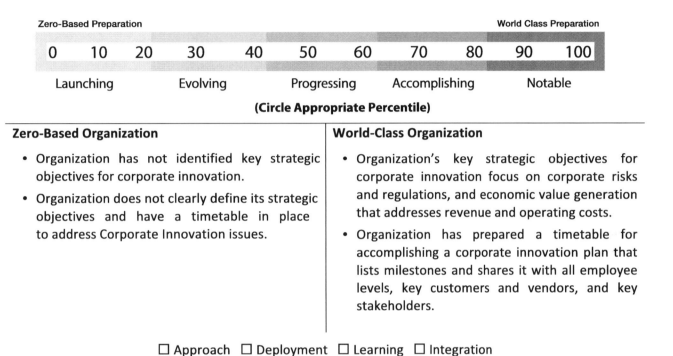

(Circle Appropriate Percentile)

Zero-Based Organization	World-Class Organization
• Organization has not identified key strategic objectives for corporate innovation. • Organization does not clearly define its strategic objectives and have a timetable in place to address Corporate Innovation issues.	• Organization's key strategic objectives for corporate innovation focus on corporate risks and regulations, and economic value generation that addresses revenue and operating costs. • Organization has prepared a timetable for accomplishing a corporate innovation plan that lists milestones and shares it with all employee levels, key customers and vendors, and key stakeholders.

☐ Approach ☐ Deployment ☐ Learning ☐ Integration

2.1b (1)   The organization's key strategic objectives for corporate innovation and timetable for accomplishing them.

+ Strengths
1.
2.
3.

- Opportunities for Improvement
1.
2.
3.

Corporate Innovation Planning Issues:
Short Term (1 to 2 years)
1.
2.

Long Term (2 years or more)
1.
2.

2.1b (2)   How does your organization address your strategic challenges and advantages for corporate innovation?

Interview notes:

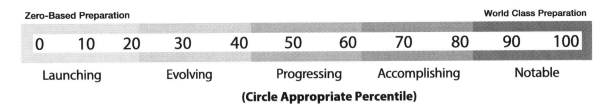

Zero-Based Preparation   **World Class Preparation**

| 0 | 10 | 20 | 30 | 40 | 50 | 60 | 70 | 80 | 90 | 100 |

Launching   Evolving   Progressing   Accomplishing   Notable

(Circle Appropriate Percentile)

Zero-Based Organization	World-Class Organization
• Organization does not align strategic objectives for corporate innovation with its short and long-term business plans and goals and ensure that key competitive marketplace issues are addressed. • Organization does not focus on strategic challenges and advantages when identifying and developing strategic objectives for corporate innovation.	• Organization ensures that its strategic objectives for corporate innovation balance the needs of all employees, key vendors, partners, and customers. • Organization addresses strategic corporate innovation objectives that are most important to the continuation of business success and overall business operations.

☐ Approach   ☐ Deployment   ☐ Learning   ☐ Integration

2.1b (2)   The organization's strategic challenges and advantages are addressed for corporate innovation.

+ Strengths

1.

2.

3.

- Opportunities for Improvement

1.

2.

3.

Corporate Innovation Planning Issues:

Short Term (1 to 2 years)

1.

2.

Long Term (2 years or more)

1.

2.

2.2 Strategy Deployment (45 pts.)

Describe how your organization converts its strategic objectives into action plans that support corporate innovation. Summarize your organization's action plans, how they are deployed, and key action plan performance measures or indicators. Project your organization's future performance relative to key comparisons on these performance measures or indicators.

QUESTIONS TO ADDRESS

2.2a (1)   What are your organization's key short and longer-term action plans for the corporate innovation?

2.2a (2)   How does your organization develop and deploy corporate innovation action plans throughout the workforce and to key vendors and partners?

2.2a (3)   How does your organization ensure that financial and other resources are available to support the accomplishment of corporate innovation action plans while meeting current obligations?

2.2a (4)   How does your organization establish and deploy modified action plans for corporate innovation?

2.2a (5)   What are your organization's key human resource plans that derive from short and longer-term corporate innovation strategic objectives and action plans?

2.2a (6)   What are your organization's key performance measures or indicators for tracking the achievement and effectiveness of corporate innovation action plans?

2.2b   What are your organization's key performance measures and projections for short and longer-term planning time horizons for corporate innovation?

2.2 Percent Score

☑ Approach   ☑ Deployment   ☑ Learning   ☑ Integration

2.2a (1)   What are your organization's key short and longer-term action plans for corporate innovation?

Interview notes:

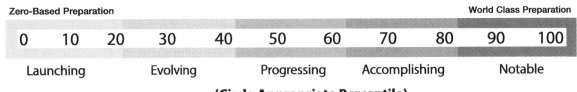

Zero-Based Preparation										World Class Preparation
0	10	20	30	40	50	60	70	80	90	100
Launching		Evolving			Progressing		Accomplishing		Notable	

(Circle Appropriate Percentile)

Zero-Based Organization	World-Class Organization
• Organization does not provide either financial or human resources to develop and deploy action plans to achieve corporate innovation goals and objectives.	• Organization's senior leadership sets and communicates corporate innovation goals, directions, and action plans to all employee levels.
• Organization has developed corporate innovation action plans but does not gauge progress toward meeting these goals.	• Organization provides financial and human resources to develop and deploy action plans to achieve key corporate innovation strategic goals and objectives.

☐ Approach   ☐ Deployment   ☐ Learning   ☐ Integration

2.2a (1)   The organization develops and deploys key short and longer-term action plans for the corporate innovation.

+ Strengths

1.

2.

3.

- Opportunities for Improvement

1.

2.

3.

Corporate Innovation Planning Issues:

Short Term (1 to 2 years)

1.

2.

Long Term (2 years or more)

1.

2.

2.2a (2)   How does your organization develop and deploy corporate innovation action plans throughout the workforce and to key vendors and partners?

Interview notes:

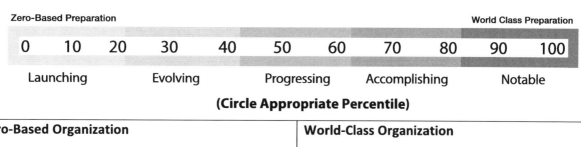

(Circle Appropriate Percentile)

Zero-Based Organization	**World-Class Organization**
• Organization has no action plans developed for corporate innovation. • Organization collects anecdotal information regarding corporate innovation efforts. Limited action plans are developed for corporate innovation and do not involve the workforce, key vendors and partners.	• Organization's key short and longer-term action plans for corporate innovation include economic, environmental, and social initiatives, and involves all workforce levels and key vendors and partners. • Organization has conducted a corporate innovation assessment that involved the workforce, key vendors, customers, and partners and developed short and long-term action plans that address key innovative opportunities identified from the assessment.

☐ Approach ☐ Deployment ☐ Learning ☐ Integration

2.2a (2)   The organization develops and deploys corporate innovation action plans throughout the workforce and to key vendors and partners.

+ Strengths

1.

2.

3.

- Opportunities for Improvement

1.

2.

3.

Corporate Innovation Planning Issues:

Short Term (1 to 2 years)

1.

2.

Long Term (2 years or more)

1.

2.

2.2a (3)   How does your organization ensure that financial and other resources are available to support the accomplishment of corporate innovation action plans while meeting current obligations?

Interview notes:

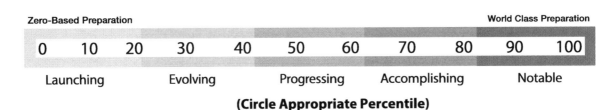

Zero-Based Preparation   World Class Preparation

| 0 | 10 | 20 | 30 | 40 | 50 | 60 | 70 | 80 | 90 | 100 |

    Launching   Evolving   Progressing   Accomplishing   Notable

(Circle Appropriate Percentile)

Zero-Based Organization	World-Class Organization
• Organization does not identify financial and/or other resources to support their corporate innovation efforts and has no formal action plans in place. • Organization is not concerned with budgeting for corporate innovation and seldom identifies other resources for staff training and leadership development opportunities for the organization.	• Organization has a formal Corporate Innovation Plan with identified financial and other resources committed to ensure accomplishment of action plans. • Organization requires all divisions to formally include budget dollars and other resources in their action plans to support corporate innovation strategic efforts.

☐ Approach   ☐ Deployment   ☐ Learning   ☐ Integration

2.2a (3)   The organization ensures that financial and other resources are available to support corporate innovation action plans while meeting current obligations.

+ Strengths

1.

2.

3.

- Opportunities for Improvement

1.

2.

3.

Corporate Innovation Planning Issues:

   Short Term (1 to 2 years)

   1.

   2.

   Long Term (2 years or more)

   1.

   2.

2.2a (4) How does your organization establish and deploy modified action plans for corporate innovation?

Interview notes:

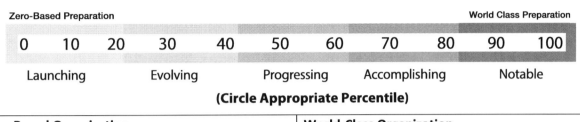

Zero-Based Preparation ... **World Class Preparation**

| 0 | 10 | 20 | 30 | 40 | 50 | 60 | 70 | 80 | 90 | 100 |

Launching   Evolving   Progressing   Accomplishing   Notable

(Circle Appropriate Percentile)

Zero-Based Organization	World-Class Organization
• Organization has no formal process in place to establish and deploy modified action plans for corporate innovation. • Organization does not modify action plans for corporate innovation. All plan changes are addressed in future planning sessions.	• Organization has an online format to establish and deploy modified action plans for corporate innovation. • All corporate innovation action plans are reviewed by selected employees, key suppliers, and customers before any modifications are made and distributed.

☐ Approach ☐ Deployment ☐ Learning ☐ Integration

2.2a (4)   the organization establishes and deploys modified action plans for corporate innovation.

+ Strengths
1.
2.
3.

- Opportunities for Improvement
1.
2.
3.

Corporate Innovation Planning Issues:

Short Term (1 to 2 years)
1.
2.

Long Term (2 years or more)
1.
2.

2.2a (5)   What are your organization's key human resource plans that derive from short and longer-term corporate innovation strategic objectives and action plans?

Interview notes:

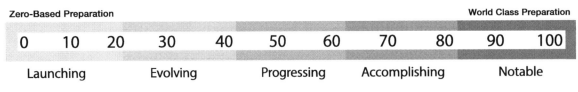

Zero-Based Preparation									World Class Preparation	
0	10	20	30	40	50	60	70	80	90	100
Launching		Evolving			Progressing		Accomplishing		Notable	

(Circle Appropriate Percentile)

Zero-Based Organization	**World-Class Organization**
• Organization does not address within their human resource plan the use of corporate innovation training and employee development services for the workforce. • Organization has not aligned its corporate innovation goals and objectives with its human resource plan.	• Organization has developed a strategic plan that addresses short and longer-term corporate innovation plans and goals for staff skills training and leadership development workshops for select employees. • Organization involves cross-functional employee teams to identify corporate innovation training/development issues and to develop a human resource plan. The plan is aligned with the organization's strategic goals and objectives.

☐ Approach   ☐ Deployment   ☐ Learning   ☐ Integration

2.2a (5)   The organization's key human resource plans derive from short and longer-term corporate innovation strategic objectives and action plans.

+ Strengths

1.

2.

3.

- Opportunities for Improvement

1.

2.

3.

Corporate Innovation Planning Issues:

Short Term (1 to 2 years)

1.

2.

Long Term (2 years or more)

1.

2.

2.2a (6)   What are your organization's key performance measures or indicators for tracking the achievement and effectiveness of corporate innovation action plans?

Interview notes:

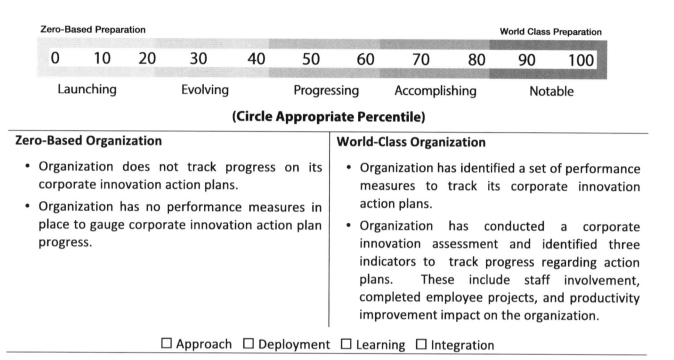

(Circle Appropriate Percentile)

Zero-Based Organization	World-Class Organization
• Organization does not track progress on its corporate innovation action plans. • Organization has no performance measures in place to gauge corporate innovation action plan progress.	• Organization has identified a set of performance measures to track its corporate innovation action plans. • Organization has conducted a corporate innovation assessment and identified three indicators to track progress regarding action plans. These include staff involvement, completed employee projects, and productivity improvement impact on the organization.

☐ Approach   ☐ Deployment   ☐ Learning   ☐ Integration

2.2a (6)   The organization's key performance measures or indicators for tracking the achievement and effectiveness of corporate innovation action plans.

+ Strengths

1.

2.

3.

- Opportunities for Improvement

1.

2.

3.

Corporate Innovation Planning Issues:

Short Term (1 to 2 years)

1.

2.

Long Term (2 years or more)

1.

2.

2.2b   What are your organization's key performance measures and projections for short and longer-term planning time horizons for corporate innovation?

Interview notes:

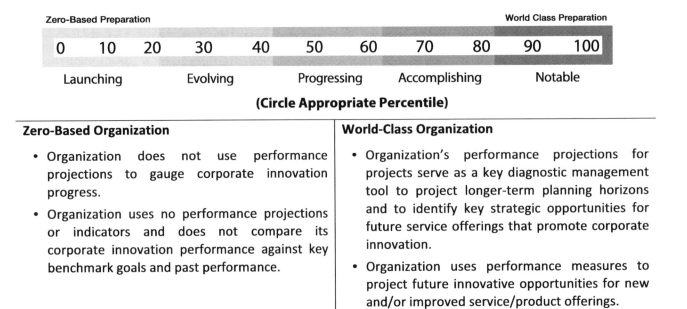

Zero-Based Preparation   **World Class Preparation**

| 0 | 10 | 20 | 30 | 40 | 50 | 60 | 70 | 80 | 90 | 100 |

Launching   Evolving   Progressing   Accomplishing   Notable

(Circle Appropriate Percentile)

Zero-Based Organization	World-Class Organization
• Organization does not use performance projections to gauge corporate innovation progress. • Organization uses no performance projections or indicators and does not compare its corporate innovation performance against key benchmark goals and past performance.	• Organization's performance projections for projects serve as a key diagnostic management tool to project longer-term planning horizons and to identify key strategic opportunities for future service offerings that promote corporate innovation. • Organization uses performance measures to project future innovative opportunities for new and/or improved service/product offerings.

☐ Approach   ☐ Deployment   ☐ Learning   ☐ Integration

2.2b   The organization's key performance measures and projections for short and longer-term planning time horizons for corporate innovation.

+ Strengths

1.

2.

3.

- Opportunities for Improvement

1.

2.

3.

Corporate Innovation Planning Issues:

Short Term (1 to 2 years)

1.

2.

Long Term (2 years or more)

1.

2.

5

Category 3
Customer Focus

3 Customer Focus (85 pts.) [26]

The Customer Focus Category examines how your organization engages its customers for long-term marketplace success and corporate innovation. This engagement strategy includes how your organization builds a customer-focused culture. Also examined is how your organization listens to the voice of its customers and uses this information to improve and identify opportunities for innovation.

3.1   Customer Engagement (40 pts.)

Describe how your organization determines innovative product/service offerings and mechanisms to support customers' use of your products/services. Describe also how your organization builds a customer-focused culture through innovation.

QUESTIONS TO ADDRESS

3.1a (1)   How does your organization identify and innovate product/service offerings to meet the requirements and exceed the expectations of your customer groups and market segments?

3.1a (2)   How does your organization determine key mechanisms to support use of products/services and enable customers to seek information and conduct business with you through innovative offerings?

3.1a(3)   How does your organization keep your approaches for identifying and innovating product/service offerings and for providing customer support current with business needs and directions?

3.1b (1)   How does your organization create a culture that ensures a consistently positive customer experience and contributes to customer engagement through innovation?

3.1b (2)   How does your organization build and manage relationships with customers through innovation?

3.1b (3)   How does your organization keep approaches for creating a customer-focused culture and keeping customer relationships current through innovation?

3.1 Percent Score

☑Approach   ☑Deployment   ☑Learning   ☑Integration

3.1a (1) How does your organization identify and innovate product/service offerings to meet the requirements and exceed the expectations of your customer groups and market segments?

Interview notes:

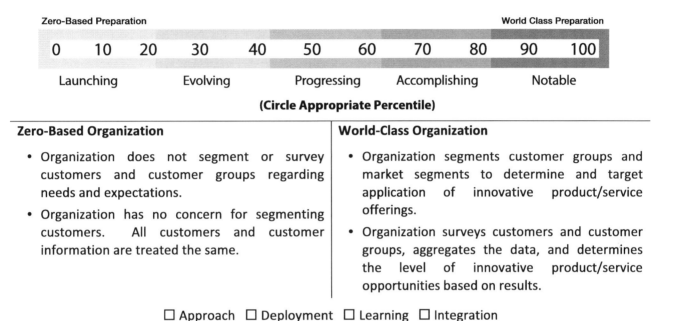

Zero-Based Preparation										World Class Preparation
0	10	20	30	40	50	60	70	80	90	100
Launching		Evolving			Progressing		Accomplishing		Notable	

(Circle Appropriate Percentile)

Zero-Based Organization	**World-Class Organization**
• Organization does not segment or survey customers and customer groups regarding needs and expectations. • Organization has no concern for segmenting customers. All customers and customer information are treated the same.	• Organization segments customer groups and market segments to determine and target application of innovative product/service offerings. • Organization surveys customers and customer groups, aggregates the data, and determines the level of innovative product/service opportunities based on results.

☐ Approach ☐ Deployment ☐ Learning ☐ Integration

3.1a (1) The organization identifies and innovates product/service offerings to meet the requirements and exceed the expectations of your customer groups and market segments.

+ Strengths
1.
2.
3.

- Opportunities for Improvement
1.
2.
3.

Corporate Innovation Planning Issues:
Short Term (1 to 2 years)
1.
2.

Long Term (2 years or more)
1.
2.

3.1a (2)   How does your organization determine key mechanisms to support use of products/services and enable customers to seek information and conduct business with you through innovative offerings?

Interview notes:

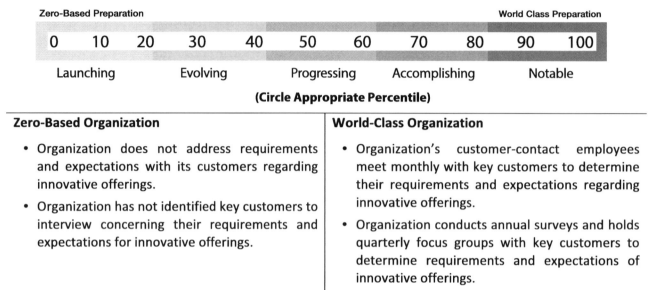

Launching   Evolving   Progressing   Accomplishing   Notable

(Circle Appropriate Percentile)

Zero-Based Organization	World-Class Organization
• Organization does not address requirements and expectations with its customers regarding innovative offerings. • Organization has not identified key customers to interview concerning their requirements and expectations for innovative offerings.	• Organization's customer-contact employees meet monthly with key customers to determine their requirements and expectations regarding innovative offerings. • Organization conducts annual surveys and holds quarterly focus groups with key customers to determine requirements and expectations of innovative offerings.

☐ Approach   ☐ Deployment   ☐ Learning   ☐ Integration

3.1a (2)   The organization determines key mechanisms to support use of products/services and enable customers to seek information, and conduct business with you through innovative offerings.

+ Strengths
1.
2.
3.

- Opportunities for Improvement
1.
2.
3.

Corporate Innovation Planning Issues:

Short Term (1 to 2 years)
1.
2.

Long Term (2 years or more)
1.
2.

3.1a (3)   How does your organization keep your approaches for identifying and innovating product/service offerings and for providing customer support current with business needs and directions?

Interview notes:

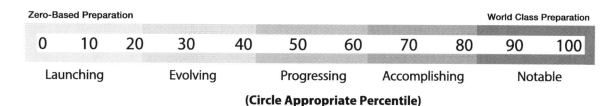

Zero-Based Preparation   **World Class Preparation**

| 0 | 10 | 20 | 30 | 40 | 50 | 60 | 70 | 80 | 90 | 100 |

Launching   Evolving   Progressing   Accomplishing   Notable

(Circle Appropriate Percentile)

Zero-Based Organization	**World-Class Organization**
• Organization is not concerned with using listening posts to better understand customer concerns and expectations. The organization has no concern for changing and incorporating innovative product/service offerings for customers. • Organization seldom changes its methods for gauging, identifying, and addressing innovative product/service offerings for customers.	• Organization annually surveys international, federal, state, and local customers and markets to ensure that listening and learning methods for its customers are current with global standards and innovative product/service offering ideas are captured. • Organization hosts annual focus groups of subject-matter experts to ensure that its customer listening and learning methods are current and state-of-the-art, and that its product/service offerings are considered to be "Best Practice" and innovative.

☐ Approach   ☐ Deployment   ☐ Learning   ☐ Integration

3.1a(3)   The organization keeps approaches for identifying and innovating product/service offerings and for providing customer support current with business needs and directions.

+ Strengths

1.

2.

3.

- Opportunities for Improvement

1.

2.

3.

Corporate Innovation Planning Issues:

Short Term (1 to 2 years)

1.

2.

Long Term (2 years or more)

1.

2.

3.1b (1)   How does your organization create a culture that ensures a consistently positive customer experience and contributes to customer engagement through innovation?

Interview notes:

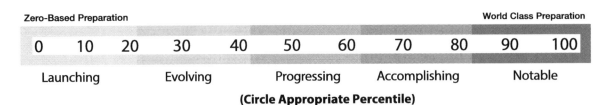

<table>
<tr><td>

Zero-Based Organization

- Organization has no formal, or consistent process in place to ensure a positive and sustainable customer experience that contributes to customer engagement through innovation.
- Organization is not concerned with customer retention and loyalty and makes limited efforts to create a sustainable customer base through innovation.

</td><td>

World-Class Organization

- Organization promotes customer engagement by involving various customer groups in brainstorming sessions to identify key ideas for innovative offerings.
- Senior management promotes their state-of-the-art technology initiatives that provide a positive customer experience derived from the use of innovative technology.

</td></tr>
</table>

☐ Approach ☐ Deployment ☐ Learning ☐ Integration

3.1b(1)   The organization creates a culture that ensures a consistently positive customer experience and contributes to customer engagement through innovation.

+ Strengths
1.
2.
3.

- Opportunities for Improvement
1.
2.
3.

Corporate Innovation Planning Issues:

Short Term (1 to 2 years)
1.
2.

Long Term (2 years or more)
1.
2.

3.1b (2)   How does your organization build and manage relationships with customers through innovation?

Interview notes:

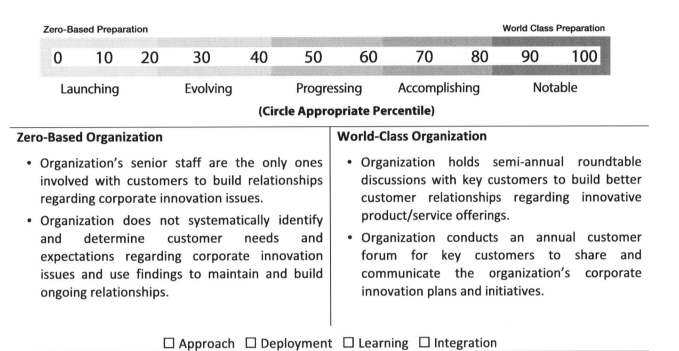

(Circle Appropriate Percentile)

Zero-Based Organization	World-Class Organization
• Organization's senior staff are the only ones involved with customers to build relationships regarding corporate innovation issues. • Organization does not systematically identify and determine customer needs and expectations regarding corporate innovation issues and use findings to maintain and build ongoing relationships.	• Organization holds semi-annual roundtable discussions with key customers to build better customer relationships regarding innovative product/service offerings. • Organization conducts an annual customer forum for key customers to share and communicate the organization's corporate innovation plans and initiatives.

☐ Approach   ☐ Deployment   ☐ Learning   ☐ Integration

3.1b (2)   The organization builds and manages relationships with customers through innovation.

+ Strengths

1.
2.
3.

- Opportunities for Improvement

1.
2.
3.

Corporate Innovation Planning Issues:

Short Term (1 to 2 years)

1.
2.

Long Term (2 years or more)

1.
2.

3.1b (3)   How does your organization keep approaches for creating a customer-focused culture and keeping customer relationships current through innovation?

Interview notes:

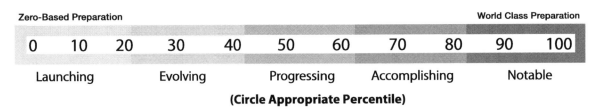

Zero-Based Preparation   World Class Preparation

| 0 | 10 | 20 | 30 | 40 | 50 | 60 | 70 | 80 | 90 | 100 |

Launching   Evolving   Progressing   Accomplishing   Notable

(Circle Appropriate Percentile)

Zero-Based Organization	World-Class Organization
• Organization is not concerned with its approach to building relationships and providing customers access to current innovative needs and directions. • Organization does not address relationship management with customers regarding corporate innovation issues and directions.	• Organization conducts formal benchmarks to organizations known to have "best practice" corporate innovation practices and approaches for customers. The organization uses its findings to validate its approaches. • Organization uses industry focus groups to review and validate its approaches to building relationships and providing customers access to corporate innovation issues and directions.

☐ Approach   ☐ Deployment   ☐ Learning   ☐ Integration

3.1b (3)   The organization keeps approaches current for creating a customer-focused culture and keeping customer relationships current through innovation.

+ Strengths

1.

2.

3.

- Opportunities for Improvement

1.

2.

3.

Corporate Innovation Planning Issues:

Short Term (1 to 2 years)

1.

2.

Long Term (2 years or more)

1.

2.

3.2 Voice of the Customer (45 pts.)

Describe how your organization listens to your customers and acquires satisfaction and dissatisfaction information. Describe also how customer information is used to improve the organization's marketplace success through innovative approaches.

QUESTIONS TO ADDRESS

3.2a (1) How does your organization obtain actionable information and feedback on your products/services and customer support and corporate innovation efforts?

3.2a (2) How does your organization listen to former customers, potential customers, and customers of competitors to obtain actionable information and to obtain feedback on products/services, customer support, and transactions and corporate innovation efforts?

3.2a (3) How does your organization manage complaints for corporate innovation efforts?

3.2b (1) How does your organization determine customer satisfaction and engagement regarding corporate innovation efforts?

3.2b (2) How does your organization obtain and use customer satisfaction data/information with corporate innovation efforts relative to their satisfaction with competitors?

3.2b (3) How does your organization determine customer dissatisfaction with corporate innovation efforts?

3.2c(1) How does your organization use customer, market, and product/service offering information to identify current and anticipate future customer groups and market segments interested in corporate innovation efforts?

3.2c(2) How does your organization use customer, market, and product/service offering information to identify and anticipate key customer requirements, changing expectations, and relative importance of corporate innovation offerings for purchasing decisions?

3.2c(3) How does your organization use customer, market, and product/service offering information to improve marketing, build a more customer-focused culture and identify opportunities for innovation?

3.2c (4) How does your organization keep approaches for customer listening, determination of customer satisfaction/dissatisfaction, and use of customer data current with corporate innovation needs and directions?

3.2 Percent Score

☑Approach ☑Deployment ☑Learning ☑Integration

3.2a (1)   How does your organization obtain actionable information and feedback on your products/services and customer support for corporate innovation efforts?

Interview notes:

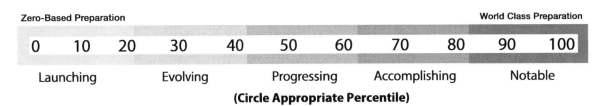

Zero-Based Preparation   World Class Preparation

| 0 | 10 | 20 | 30 | 40 | 50 | 60 | 70 | 80 | 90 | 100 |

Launching   Evolving   Progressing   Accomplishing   Notable

(Circle Appropriate Percentile)

Zero-Based Organization	World-Class Organization
• Organization performs limited follow-up with customers on product/service offerings and receives little feedback on the organization's corporate innovation efforts. • Organization does not engage customers through focus groups, surveys, complaint data, and information and use to validate ongoing satisfaction with corporate innovation efforts and to make actionable charges.	• Organization uses focus groups and customer appreciation councils to obtain information and feedback on products/ services and customer support for corporate innovation efforts. • Organization uses several feedback modes to gauge customer satisfaction with corporate innovation efforts as they relate to product/ service offerings which include focus groups with key customers, interviews with lost and potential customers, customer complaint data, and a win/loss analysis relative to competitors who offer similar products/ services.

☐ Approach   ☐ Deployment   ☐ Learning   ☐ Integration

3.2a (1)   The organization obtains actionable information and feedback on products/services and customer support for corporate innovation efforts.

+ Strengths

1.
2.
3.

- Opportunities for Improvement

1.
2.
3.

Corporate Innovation Planning Issues:

Short Term (1 to 2 years)

1.
2.

Long Term (2 years or more)

1.
2.

3.2a (2)   How does your organization listen to former customers, potential customers, and customers of competitors to obtain actionable information and to obtain feedback on products/services, customer support, and transactions for corporate innovation efforts?

Interview notes:

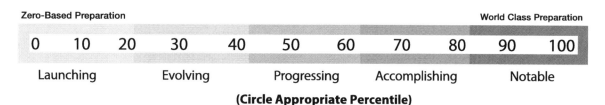

Zero-Based Preparation										World Class Preparation
0	10	20	30	40	50	60	70	80	90	100
Launching		Evolving			Progressing		Accomplishing		Notable	

(Circle Appropriate Percentile)

Zero-Based Organization	**World-Class Organization**
• Organization has no formal process in place to seek and review feedback from former customers, potential customers, and customers of competitors. • Organization is not concerned with receiving feedback from former customers, potential customers, and customers of competitors and using feedback information to gauge product/service satisfaction to identify customer support issues and to improve corporate innovation efforts.	• Organization conducts focus groups with former customers, potential customers, and customers of competitors. Data and information is used to gauge their overall concerns with product/ services, and customer support for corporate innovation efforts. • Organization surveys all former customers, potential customers, and customers of competitors to gauge to what extent corporate innovation offerings are important to them in purchasing products/services.

☐ Approach ☐ Deployment ☐ Learning ☐ Integration

3.2a (2)   The organization listens to former customers, potential customers, and customers of competitors to obtain feedback on products/services, customer support and transactions for corporate innovation efforts.

+ Strengths

1.

2.

3.

- Opportunities for Improvement

1.

2.

3.

Corporate Innovation Planning Issues:

Short Term (1 to 2 years)

1.

2.

Long Term (2 years or more)

1.

2.

3.2a (3)   How does your organization manage complaints for corporate innovation efforts?

Interview notes:

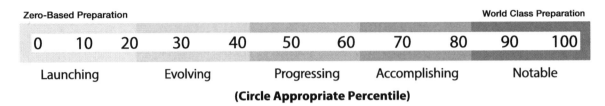

Zero-Based Preparation   World Class Preparation

| 0 | 10 | 20 | 30 | 40 | 50 | 60 | 70 | 80 | 90 | 100 |

Launching   Evolving   Progressing   Accomplishing   Notable

(Circle Appropriate Percentile)

Zero-Based Organization	World-Class Organization
• Organization does not have a dedicated 24-hour mechanism in place to address customer's requests, concerns, and complaints regarding corporate innovation initiatives. • Organization does not have a process in place for customers to seek information, conduct business, and register corporate innovation complaints.	• Organization has a 24-hour, 1-800 phone line and help desk to address corporate innovation issues and complaints. In addition, a Chief Innovation Officer (CIO) is in place to address customer concerns. • Organization has a customer website devoted to corporate innovation issues. The website allows customers to seek information, conduct business, and register complaints regarding corporate innovation issues and concerns twenty-four hours a day seven days a week. All complaints are responded to within 8 hours.

☐ Approach   ☐ Deployment   ☐ Learning   ☐ Integration

3.2a (3)   The organization manages complaints for corporate innovation efforts.

+ Strengths
1.
2.
3.

- Opportunities for Improvement
1.
2.
3.

Corporate Innovation Planning Issues:

Short Term (1 to 2 years)
1.
2.

Long Term (2 years or more)
1.
2.

3.2b (1)   How does your organization determine customer satisfaction and engagement regarding corporate innovation efforts?

Interview notes:

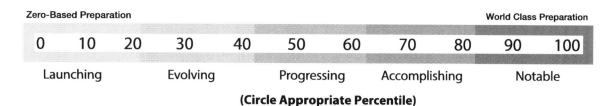

Launching   Evolving   Progressing   Accomplishing   Notable

(Circle Appropriate Percentile)

Zero-Based Organization	**World-Class Organization**
• Organization has no processes in place to determine customer satisfaction/ dissatisfaction with corporate innovation issues and initiatives.	• Organization surveys customers annually to determine their satisfaction/ dissatisfaction with corporate innovation initiatives.
• Organization collects customer satisfaction/ dissatisfaction data regarding corporate innovation issues, but does not aggregate data and use to identify areas for process improvements.	• Organization hosts a blue-ribbon customer panel annually to document its overall satisfaction / dissatisfaction with corporate innovation initiatives. Findings are aggregated by market segments and used for process improvement.

☐ Approach   ☐ Deployment   ☐ Learning   ☐ Integration

3.2b (1)   The organization determines customer satisfaction and engagement regarding corporate innovation efforts.

+ Strengths

1.

2.

3.

- Opportunities for Improvement

1.

2.

3.

Corporate Innovation Planning Issues:

Short Term (1 to 2 years)

1.

2.

Long Term (2 years or more)

1.

2.

3.2b (2)   How does your organization obtain and use customer satisfaction data/information with corporate innovation efforts relative to their satisfaction with competitors?

Interview notes:

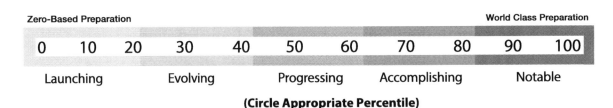

Zero-Based Preparation   World Class Preparation

| 0 | 10 | 20 | 30 | 40 | 50 | 60 | 70 | 80 | 90 | 100 |

Launching   Evolving   Progressing   Accomplishing   Notable

(Circle Appropriate Percentile)

Zero-Based Organization	World-Class Organization
• Organization does not use comparison and benchmark data to gauge customer satisfaction with the organization's corporate innovation initiatives. • Organization's data comparisons regarding customer satisfaction with corporate innovation initiatives relative to the organization's competition appears anecdotal.	• Organization uses benchmark and comparison data to improve its corporate innovation initiatives with customers. • Organization conducts quarterly satisfaction surveys with key customers to gauge their satisfaction with corporate innovation efforts relative to their satisfaction with their competitors.

☐ Approach   ☐ Deployment   ☐ Learning   ☐ Integration

3.2b (2)   The organization obtains and uses customer satisfaction data/information with corporate innovation efforts relative to their satisfaction with competitors.

+ Strengths

1.
2.
3.

- Opportunities for Improvement

1.
2.
3.

Corporate Innovation Planning Issues:

Short Term (1 to 2 years)

1.
2.

Long Term (2 years or more)

1.
2.

3.2b (3)   How does your organization determine customer dissatisfaction with corporate innovation efforts?

Interview notes:

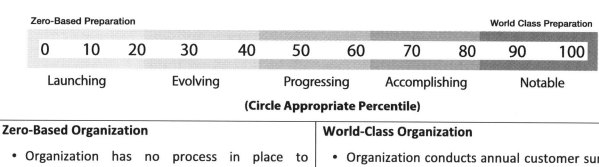

(Circle Appropriate Percentile)

Zero-Based Organization	**World-Class Organization**
• Organization has no process in place to determine if customer satisfaction with the organization's approach regarding corporate innovation issues and initiatives is current and addresses their needs and directions. • Organization is not concerned with gauging the currency of its approach to determine customer satisfaction with corporate innovation offerings.	• Organization conducts annual customer surveys to ensure that corporate innovation initiatives offered to customers are current with their strategic needs and directions. • Customer focus groups are conducted biannually to gauge to what extent the organization's approaches for determining customer satisfaction/dissatisfaction with corporate innovation efforts is meeting their needs and helping to identify areas of dissatisfaction.

☐ Approach ☐ Deployment ☐ Learning ☐ Integration

3.2b (3)   The organization determines customer dissatisfaction with corporate innovation efforts.

+ Strengths

1.

2.

3.

- Opportunities for Improvement

1.

2.

3.

Corporate Innovation Planning Issues:

Short Term (1 to 2 years)

1.

2.

Long Term (2 years or more)

1.

2.

3.2c(1)   How does your organization use customer, market, and product/service offering information to identify current and anticipate future customer groups and market segments interested in corporate innovation efforts?

Interview notes:

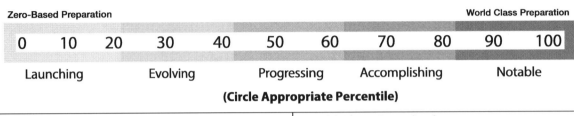

(Circle Appropriate Percentile)

Zero-Based Organization	World-Class Organization
• Organization does not have a process in place to obtain information from customers and market segments to gauge their interests in corporate innovation efforts and initiatives. • Organization has no interest in gauging customer interest in corporate innovation efforts.	• Organization surveys key customer groups and conducts focus groups and community forums to identify customers and market segments interested in corporate innovation offerings. • Organization has developed a corporate innovation plan based on customer and market survey results and product/service offering information.

☐ Approach ☐ Deployment ☐ Learning ☐ Integration

3.2c(1)   The organization uses customer, market, and product/service offering information to identify current and anticipate future customer groups and market segments interested in corporate innovation efforts.

+ Strengths

1.

2.

3.

- Opportunities for Improvement

1.

2.

3.

Corporate Innovation Planning Issues:

Short Term (1 to 2 years)

1.

2.

Long Term (2 years or more)

1.

2.

3.2c(2)   How does your organization use customer, market, and product/service offering information to identify and anticipate key customer requirements, changing expectations, and relative importance of corporate innovation offerings for purchasing decisions?

Interview notes:

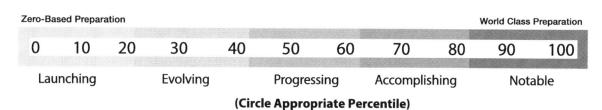

Zero-Based Preparation   **World Class Preparation**

| 0 | 10 | 20 | 30 | 40 | 50 | 60 | 70 | 80 | 90 | 100 |

Launching   Evolving   Progressing   Accomplishing   Notable

(Circle Appropriate Percentile)

Zero-Based Organization	World-Class Organization
• Organization does not use customer, market and product/service offering information to identify purchasing decisions based on corporate innovation efforts.	• Organization addresses customer, market, and product/service offering data and information in its Corporate Innovation Plan to increase customer purchasing decisions.
• Organization has no interest in using market data/information to determine customers interest in making increased purchasing decisions for corporate innovation offerings.	• Organization incorporates customer, market and product/service offering information to identify key products/services to be considered in its corporate innovation plan.

□ Approach   □ Deployment   □ Learning   □ Integration

3.2c (2)   The organization uses customer, market and product/service offering information to identify and anticipate key customer requirements, changing expectations, and relative importance of corporate innovation offerings for purchasing decisions.

+ Strengths

1.

2.

3.

- Opportunities for Improvement

1.

2.

3.

Corporate Innovation Planning Issues:

Short Term (1 to 2 years)

1.

2.

Long Term (2 years or more)

1.

2.

3.2c(3)   How does your organization use customer, market, and product/service offering information to improve marketing, build a more customer-focused culture and identify opportunities for innovation?

Interview notes:

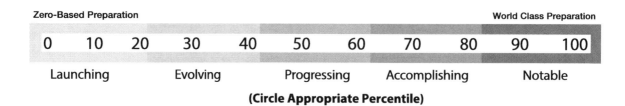

Launching   Evolving   Progressing   Accomplishing   Notable

(Circle Appropriate Percentile)

Zero-Based Organization	World-Class Organization
• Organization does not use customer, market and product/service offering information to identify innovative efforts to improve customer service and purchases. • Organization does not consider using customer, market and product/service offering information to gauge what impact the organization's corporate innovation efforts are having on customer satisfaction and increased purchases.	• Organization uses customer, market, and product/service offering information to better understand factors that drive corporate innovation and impacts competitiveness in product/service offerings. • Organization incorporates customer, market, and product/service offering information to identify opportunities to increase sales based on their innovative corporate efforts.

☐ Approach   ☐ Deployment   ☐ Learning   ☐ Integration

3.2c(3)   The organization uses customer, market, and product/service offering information to improve marketing, build a more customer-focused culture, and identify opportunities for innovation.

+ Strengths

1.

2.

3.

- Opportunities for Improvement

1.

2.

3.

Corporate Innovation Planning Issues:

Short Term (1 to 2 years)

1.

2.

Long Term (2 years or more)

1.

2.

3.2c (4)   How does your organization keep approaches for customer listening, determination of customer satisfaction/dissatisfaction, and use of customer data current with corporate innovation needs and directions?

Interview notes:

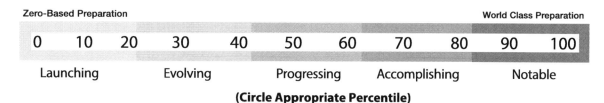

Zero-Based Preparation   World Class Preparation

| 0 | 10 | 20 | 30 | 40 | 50 | 60 | 70 | 80 | 90 | 100 |

Launching   Evolving   Progressing   Accomplishing   Notable

(Circle Appropriate Percentile)

Zero-Based Organization	**World-Class Organization**
• Organization does not review customer satisfaction/ dissatisfaction data to gauge to what extent it is current with corporate innovation needs and directions. • Organization does not use customer data and information to determine current and future directions for corporate innovation.	• Organization uses customer data and listening posts to ensure that corporate innovation efforts are current and helping to drive customer satisfaction and loyalty. • Organization uses their website to receive customer input and to ensure that all corporate innovation efforts are current and meeting and/or exceeding customer expectations and concerns.

☐ Approach   ☐ Deployment   ☐ Learning   ☐ Integration

3.2c (4)   The organization keeps approaches for customer listening, determination of customer satisfaction/dissatisfaction, and use of customer data current with corporate innovation needs and directions.

+ Strengths

1.
2.
3.

- Opportunities for Improvement

1.
2.
3.

Corporate Innovation Planning Issues:

Short Term (1 to 2 years)

1.
2.

Long Term (2 years or more)

1.
2.

NOTES

6

Category 4
Measurement, Analysis, and
Knowledge Management

4 Measurement, Analysis, and Knowledge Management (90 pts.) [27]

The Measurement, Analysis, and Knowledge Management Category examines how your organization selects, gathers, analyzes, manages, and improves data, information, and knowledge assets and how it manages information technology that is related to corporate innovation. The Category also examines how your organization examines and uses reviews to improve the overall performance of corporate innovation.

4.1   Measurement, Analysis, and Improvement of Organizational Performance   (45 pts.)

PROCESS

Describe how your organization measures, analyzes, reviews, and improves corporate innovation performance through the use of data and information at all levels and in all parts of your organization.

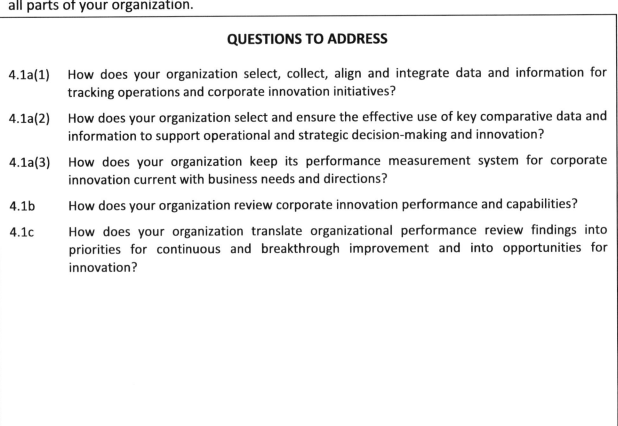

QUESTIONS TO ADDRESS

4.1a(1)   How does your organization select, collect, align and integrate data and information for tracking operations and corporate innovation initiatives?

4.1a(2)   How does your organization select and ensure the effective use of key comparative data and information to support operational and strategic decision-making and innovation?

4.1a(3)   How does your organization keep its performance measurement system for corporate innovation current with business needs and directions?

4.1b   How does your organization review corporate innovation performance and capabilities?

4.1c   How does your organization translate organizational performance review findings into priorities for continuous and breakthrough improvement and into opportunities for innovation?

4.1 Percent Score

☑ Approach   ☑ Deployment   ☑ Learning   ☑ Integration

4.1a (1)   How does your organization select, collect, align and integrate data and information for tracking operations and corporate innovation initiatives?

Interview notes:

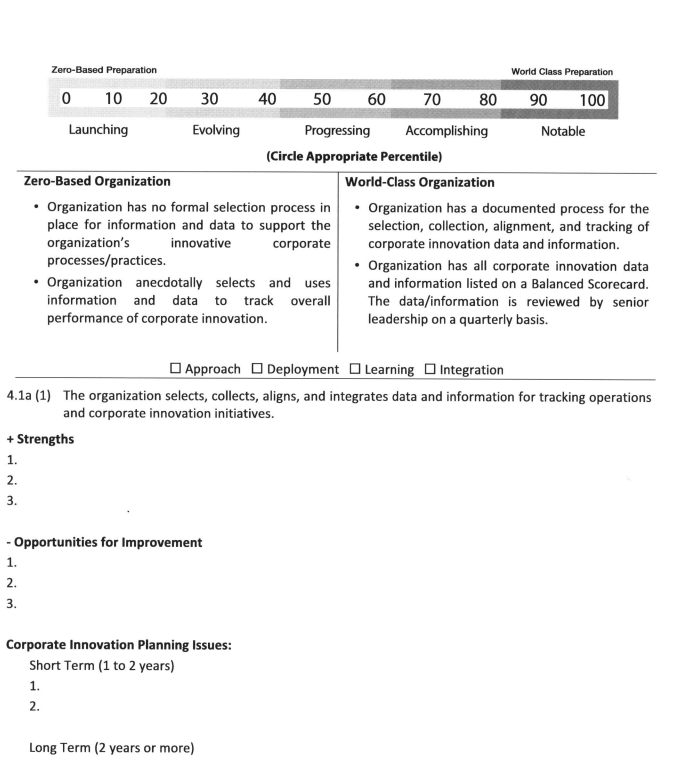

Zero-Based Preparation | World Class Preparation

0   10   20   30   40   50   60   70   80   90   100

Launching   Evolving   Progressing   Accomplishing   Notable

(Circle Appropriate Percentile)

Zero-Based Organization	World-Class Organization
• Organization has no formal selection process in place for information and data to support the organization's innovative corporate processes/practices. • Organization anecdotally selects and uses information and data to track overall performance of corporate innovation.	• Organization has a documented process for the selection, collection, alignment, and tracking of corporate innovation data and information. • Organization has all corporate innovation data and information listed on a Balanced Scorecard. The data/information is reviewed by senior leadership on a quarterly basis.

☐ Approach   ☐ Deployment   ☐ Learning   ☐ Integration

4.1a (1)   The organization selects, collects, aligns, and integrates data and information for tracking operations and corporate innovation initiatives.

+ Strengths

1.

2.

3.

- Opportunities for Improvement

1.

2.

3.

Corporate Innovation Planning Issues:

Short Term (1 to 2 years)

1.

2.

Long Term (2 years or more)

1.

2.

4.1a (2)   How does your organization select and ensure the effective use of key comparative data and information to support operational and strategic decision making and innovation?

Interview notes:

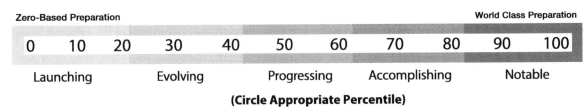

Zero-Based Preparation   World Class Preparation

| 0 | 10 | 20 | 30 | 40 | 50 | 60 | 70 | 80 | 90 | 100 |

Launching   Evolving   Progressing   Accomplishing   Notable

(Circle Appropriate Percentile)

Zero-Based Organization	World-Class Organization
• Organization does not use comparative data and information to support corporate innovation decision making and short and longer-term strategic planning. • Organization makes no comparisons against other organizations known for their innovative practices.	• Organization selects data/information by reviewing organizations that exhibit innovative practices. The selected data and information are compared against industry organizations, known for their notable practices, and used to support strategic decision making throughout the organization. • Organization has published a corporate innovation data and information guide to support operational and strategic decision-making and to secure the organization's sustainability and competiveness.

☐ Approach   ☐ Deployment   ☐ Learning   ☐ Integration

4.1a (2)   The organization selects and ensures the effective use of key comparative data and information to support operational and strategic decision making and innovation.

+ Strengths

1.

2.

3.

- Opportunities for Improvement

1.

2.

3.

Corporate Innovation Planning Issues:

Economic

1.

2.

Long Term (2 years or more)

1.

2.

4.1a (3)   How does your organization keep its performance measurement system for corporate innovation current with business needs and directions?

Interview notes:

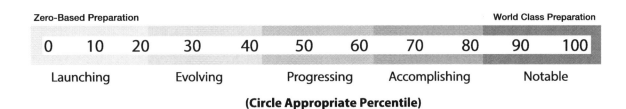

Zero-Based Preparation   World Class Preparation

| 0 | 10 | 20 | 30 | 40 | 50 | 60 | 70 | 80 | 90 | 100 |

Launching   Evolving   Progressing   Accomplishing   Notable

(Circle Appropriate Percentile)

Zero-Based Organization	World-Class Organization
• Organization does nothing to keep its performance measurement system for corporate innovation current with business needs and directions.	• Organization reviews its performance measurement system and corporate innovation annually to ensure it remains current with business needs and directions.
• Organization has no process in place to ensure that its performance measurement system for corporate innovation is timely and sensitive to unexpected external, environmental, financial, and/or social changes.	• Organization ensures that its performance measurement system and corporate innovation is sensitive to rapid and unexpected environmental, financial, and social changes.

☐ Approach ☐ Deployment ☐ Learning ☐ Integration

4.1a (3)   The organization's performance measurement system for corporate innovation is kept current with business needs and directions.

+ Strengths

1.

2.

3.

- Opportunities for Improvement

1.

2.

3.

Corporate Innovation Planning Issues:

Short Term (1 to 2 years)

1.

2.

Long Term (2 years or more)

1.

2.

4.1b   How does your organization review corporate innovation performance and capabilities?

Interview notes:

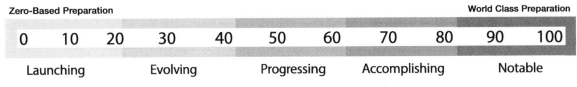

Zero-Based Preparation   World Class Preparation

| 0 | 10 | 20 | 30 | 40 | 50 | 60 | 70 | 80 | 90 | 100 |

Launching   Evolving   Progressing   Accomplishing   Notable

(Circle Appropriate Percentile)

Zero-Based Organization	**World-Class Organization**
• Organization uses anecdotal data to support organizational reviews of corporate innovation performance and capabilities. • Organization does not analyze data and information to support performance and capability review of corporate innovation.	• Organization uses "best practice" benchmark data and information to support organizational performance and capability reviews for key corporate innovation initiatives. • Organization has developed Service Quality Indicators (SQIs) for key corporate innovation initiatives and reviews the indicators on a monthly basis to gauge performance and capability.

☐ Approach   ☐ Deployment   ☐ Learning   ☐ Integration

4.1b   The organization reviews corporate innovation performance and capability.

+ Strengths

1.
2.
3.

- Opportunities for Improvement

1.
2.
3.

Corporate Innovation Planning Issues:

Short Term (1 to 2 years)

1.
2.

Long Term (2 years or more)

1.
2.

4.1c   How does your organization translate organizational performance review findings into priorities for continuous and breakthrough improvement and into opportunities for innovation?

Interview notes:

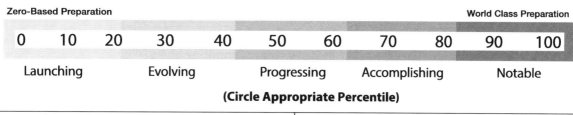

Zero-Based Preparation   **World Class Preparation**

| 0 | 10 | 20 | 30 | 40 | 50 | 60 | 70 | 80 | 90 | 100 |

Launching   Evolving   Progressing   Accomplishing   Notable

(Circle Appropriate Percentile)

Zero-Based Organization	**World-Class Organization**
• Organization's corporate innovation data are neither linked, nor supportive of work-group and functional-level decision making. • Organization does not communicate corporate innovation data and information to employees, suppliers, partners, and customers.	• Organization's corporate innovation data and information is user-friendly and presented in vivid graphs and charts to support functional-level decision-making. • Organization communicates organizational results through its online newsletters to employees, suppliers, partners, and customers. The newsletters are provided to promote breakthrough thinking and improvement in corporate innovation efforts.

☐ Approach   ☐ Deployment   ☐ Learning   ☐ Integration

4.1c   The organization translates organizational performance review findings into priorities for continuous and breakthrough improvement and into opportunities for innovation.

+ Strengths

1.

2.

3.

- Opportunities for Improvement

1.

2.

3.

Corporate Innovation Planning Issues:

Short Term (1 to 2 years)

1.

2.

Long Term (2 years or more)

1.

2.

4.2   Management of Information, Knowledge, and Information Technology (45 pts.)

PROCESS

Describe how your organization ensures the quality and availability of needed data, information, software, and hardware for your workforce, suppliers, partners, collaborators, and customers.   Describe how your organization builds and manages its corporate innovation assets.

QUESTIONS TO ADDRESS

4.2(a) 1   How does your organization ensure that its corporate innovation data, information, and knowledge are accurate, have integrity and reliability, and are timely, secure, and confidential?

4.2a (2)   How does your organization ensure that needed corporate innovation data and information is available to your workforce, suppliers, partners, collaborators, and customers?

4.2a(3)   How does your organization collect and transfer relevant organizational knowledge and sharing of innovative best practices from employees, customers, suppliers, partners, and collaborators to use in your strategic planning process?

4.2b (1)   How does your organization ensure that hardware and software supporting corporate innovation is reliable, secure, and user-friendly?

4.2b (2)   How does your organization ensure the continued availability of hardware/software systems and the continued availability and security of corporate innovation data and information in the event of an emergency?

4.2b(3)   How does your organization keep data and information availability mechanisms that support corporate innovation, including software and hardware systems, current with business needs and directions and technological changes?

4.2 Percent Score

☑Approach   ☑Deployment   ☑Learning   ☑Integration

4.2(a) 1   How does your organization ensure that its corporate innovation data, information, and knowledge are accurate, have integrity and reliability, and are timely, secure, and confidential?

Interview notes:

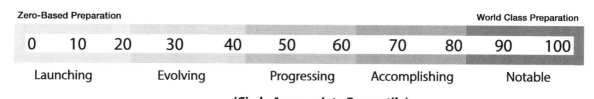

Zero-Based Preparation   World Class Preparation

| 0 | 10 | 20 | 30 | 40 | 50 | 60 | 70 | 80 | 90 | 100 |

Launching   Evolving   Progressing   Accomplishing   Notable

(Circle Appropriate Percentile)

Zero-Based Organization	World-Class Organization
• Organization has no process in place to ensure that corporate innovation data and knowledge management are reliable, protected, timely, and secure. • Organization has no ongoing systems in place to review and ensure that corporate innovation data, information, and organizational knowledge are maintained properly.	• Organization surveys data users bi-monthly to ensure that corporate innovation data and knowledge management have integrity, timeliness, reliability, security, accuracy, and confidentiality. • Organization's corporate innovation data, information, and organizational knowledge are reviewed weekly to ensure that it is reliable, protected, timely, and secure.

☐ Approach   ☐ Deployment   ☐ Learning   ☐ Integration

4.2a (1)   The organization ensures that its corporate innovation data, information, and knowledge are accurate, have integrity and reliability, and are secure and confidential.

+ Strengths
1.
2.
3.

- Opportunities for Improvement
1.
2.
3.

Corporate Innovation Planning Issues:

Short Term (1 to 2 years)
1.
2.

Long Term (2 years or more)
1.
2.

4.2a (2)   How does your organization ensure that needed corporate innovation data and information are available to your workforce, suppliers, partners, collaborators, and customers?

Interview notes:

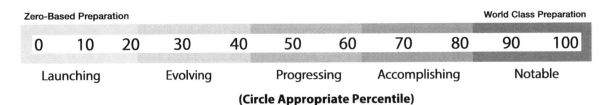

(Circle Appropriate Percentile)

Zero-Based Organization	World-Class Organization
• Organization does not have a consistent and reliable method for deploying corporate innovation data and information to various stakeholders. • Organization sends corporate innovation data and information on a "request only" basis to employees, suppliers, partners, and customers.	• Organization uses a subscriber website to deploy needed corporate innovation data and information to the workforce, suppliers, partners, collaborators, and customers. • Organization has a dedicated team to dispense corporate innovation data and information to suppliers, partners, and customers on a monthly basis.

☐ Approach ☐ Deployment ☐ Learning ☐ Integration

4.2a (2)   The organization ensures that needed corporate innovation data and information are available to the workforce, suppliers, partners, collaborators, and customers.

+ Strengths

1.

2.

3.

- Opportunities for Improvement

1.

2.

3.

Corporate Innovation Planning Issues:

Short Term (1 to 2 years)

1.

2.

Long Term (2 years or more)

1.

2.

4.2a(3)   How does your organization collect and transfer relevant organizational knowledge and sharing of innovative best practices from employees, customers, suppliers, partners, and collaborators to use in your strategic planning process?

Interview notes:

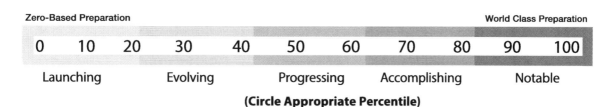

Zero-Based Organization

- Organization has no systematic methodology in place to manage, collect, and transfer corporate innovation knowledge.
- Organization collects data and information, but has no system in place to store and transfer corporate innovation knowledge to stakeholder groups.

World-Class Organization

- Organization has a software system in place that manages, collects, and transfers corporate innovation data/information and knowledge to employees, suppliers, partners, and customers. The data is used to identify strategic opportunities to ensure timely transfer of relevant organizational knowledge to the workforce and various stakeholder groups.
- Organization has an online knowledge management system for corporate innovation that is accessible to employees, suppliers, partners, customers, and collaborators.

☐ Approach ☐ Deployment ☐ Learning ☐ Integration

4.2a(3)   The organization collects and transfers relevant organizational knowledge and sharing of innovative best practices from employees, customers, suppliers, partners, and collaborators to use in your strategic planning process.

+ Strengths
1.
2.
3.

- Opportunities for Improvement
1.
2.
3.

Corporate Innovation Planning Issues:
   Short Term (1 to 2 years)
   1.
   2.

   Long Term (2 years or more)
   1.
   2.

4.2b (1)   How does your organization ensure that hardware and software supporting corporate innovation are reliable, secure, and user-friendly?

Interview notes:

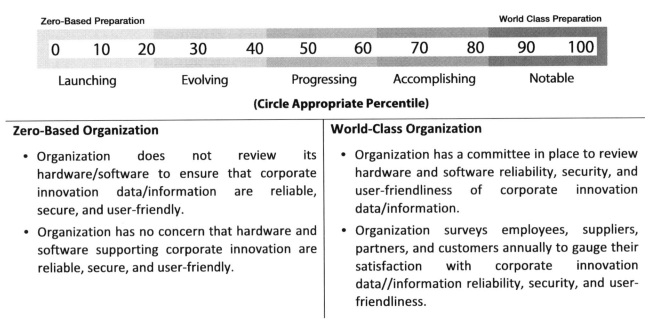

Zero-Based Organization	World-Class Organization
• Organization does not review its hardware/software to ensure that corporate innovation data/information are reliable, secure, and user-friendly. • Organization has no concern that hardware and software supporting corporate innovation are reliable, secure, and user-friendly.	• Organization has a committee in place to review hardware and software reliability, security, and user-friendliness of corporate innovation data/information. • Organization surveys employees, suppliers, partners, and customers annually to gauge their satisfaction with corporate innovation data//information reliability, security, and user-friendliness.

☐ Approach ☐ Deployment ☐ Learning ☐ Integration

4.2b (1)   The organization ensures that hardware and software supporting corporate innovation is reliable, secure, and user-friendly.

+ Strengths

1.
2.
3.

- Opportunities for Improvement

1.
2.
3.

Corporate Innovation Planning Issues:

Short Term (1 to 2 years)

1.
2.

Long Term (2 years or more)

1.
2.

4.2b (2)   How does your organization ensure the continued availability of hardware/software systems and the continued availability and security of corporate innovation data and information in the event of an emergency?

Interview notes:

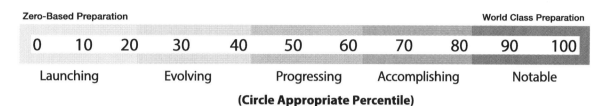

Zero-Based Preparation   World Class Preparation

| 0 | 10 | 20 | 30 | 40 | 50 | 60 | 70 | 80 | 90 | 100 |

Launching   Evolving   Progressing   Accomplishing   Notable

(Circle Appropriate Percentile)

Zero-Based Organization	**World-Class Organization**
• Organization has no formal process in place to ensure hardware/software availability and security of corporate innovation data and information in the event of an emergency.	• Organization has a formal Business Continuity Plan in place that addresses protection of corporate innovation data and information in the event of an emergency.
• Organization has no concern for protecting corporate innovation data and information in the event of an emergency.	• Organization has developed a dedicated website for all corporate innovation data and information that is password-protected and can be accessed by the workforce, key customers, suppliers, and collaborators in the event of an emergency.

☐ Approach   ☐ Deployment   ☐ Learning   ☐ Integration

4.2b (2)   The organization ensures the continued availability of hardware/software systems and the continued availability of corporate innovation data and information in the event of an emergency.

+ Strengths

1.

2.

3.

- Opportunities for Improvement

1.

2.

3.

Corporate Innovation Planning Issues:

Short Term (1 to 2 years)

1.

2.

Long Term (2 years or more)

1.

2.

4.2b(3)   How does your organization keep data and information availability mechanisms that support corporate innovation, including software and hardware systems, current with business needs and directions and technological changes?

Interview notes:

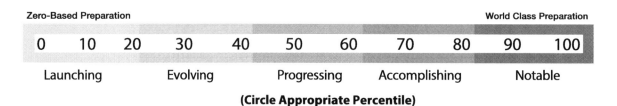

(Circle Appropriate Percentile)

Zero-Based Organization	World-Class Organization
• Organization has no infrastructure in place to support and secure information networks for corporate innovation. • Organization has little concern that systems are in place to support and secure corporate innovation data and information.	• Organization benchmarks notable "best practice" information systems that support corporate innovation to ensure that its system is secure and is current with business needs and directions and technological changes. • Organization has in place a corporate innovation data support team to ensure that software/hardware systems and technology are secure and current with the organization's operational needs.

☐ Approach   ☐ Deployment   ☐ Learning   ☐ Integration

4.2b(3)   The organization keeps data and information availability mechanisms that support corporate innovation, including software and hardware systems, current with business needs and directions and technological changes.

+ Strengths

1.

2.

3.

- Opportunities for Improvement

1.

2.

3.

Corporate Innovation Planning Issues:

   Short Term (1 to 2 years)

   1.

   2.

   Long Term (2 years or more)

   1.

   2.

7 Category 5 Workforce Focus

5 Workforce Focus (85 pts.) [28]

The Workforce Focus Category examines how your organization assesses workforce capability and capacity needs and builds a workforce environment conducive to high performance and innovative practices. The category also asks how your organization engages, manages, and develops your workforce to utilize its full potential in alignment with your organization's overall organization needs.

5.1   Workforce Engagement   (45 pts.)

Describe how your organization engages, and rewards your workforce to achieve high performance and innovation. Describe how members of your workforce, including leaders, are developed to achieve high performance. Describe how you assess workforce engagement and use the results to achieve higher performance and innovation.

QUESTIONS TO ADDRESS

5.1a (1)   How does your organization determine key factors that affect workforce engagement as it relates to corporate innovation?

5.1a (2)   How does your organization's culture promote open communication, high performance work and an engaged workforce that benefits from diverse ideas, cultures, and thinking as they relate to corporate innovation?

5.1a (3)   How does your organization's workforce performance management system support corporate innovation initiatives within the organization and reward, recognize, and compensate the workforce for reinforcing a customer and business focus and achievement of your action plans?

5.1b (1)   How does your organization's learning and development system address core competencies, strategic challenges, accomplishment of its action plans, performance improvement, ethics, training, coaching, mentoring and work-related experiences as they relate to corporate innovation?

5.1b (2)   How does your organization's workforce learning and development system address transfer of knowledge from departing or retiring workers and reinforce new knowledge and skills on the job as they relate to corporate innovation?

5.1b (3)   How does your organization evaluate the effectiveness and efficiency of its learning and development systems and ensure consistency as they relate to corporate innovation?

5.1b (4)   How does your organization manage effective career progression and accomplish effective succession planning for management and leadership positions as they relate to corporate innovation?

5.1c (1)   How does your organization assess workforce engagement as it relates to corporate innovation?

5.1c (2)   How does your organization align workforce engagement assessment findings to key business results as they relate to corporate innovation?

5.1 Percent Score

☑Approach   ☑Deployment   ☑Learning   ☑Integration

5.1a (1)   How does your organization determine key factors that affect workforce engagement as it relates to corporate innovation?

Interview notes:

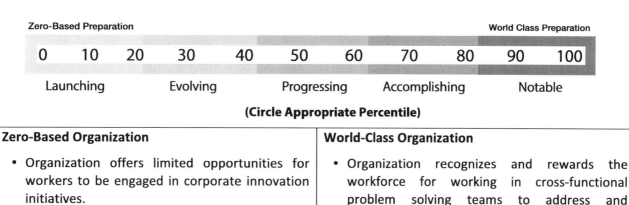

Zero-Based Organization	World-Class Organization
• Organization offers limited opportunities for workers to be engaged in corporate innovation initiatives. • Organization does not allow employees to review and discuss innovative practices and issues on company time. Workers who engage in discussing corporate innovation issues are disciplined.	• Organization recognizes and rewards the workforce for working in cross-functional problem solving teams to address and ultimately help solve corporate issues based on innovative solutions. • Organization rewards workers who are engaged in corporate innovation issues and solutions with a year-end bonus plan.

☐ Approach ☐ Deployment ☐ Learning ☐ Integration

5.1a (1)   The organization determines key factors that affect workforce engagement as it relates to corporate innovation.

+ Strengths

1.
2.
3.

- Opportunities for Improvement

1.
2.
3.

Corporate Innovation Planning Issues:

Short Term (1 to 2 years)

1.
2.

Long Term (2 years or more)

1.
2.

5.1a(2)   How does your organization's culture promote open communication, high performance work and an engaged workforce that benefits from diverse ideas, cultures, and thinking as they relate to corporate innovation?

Interview notes:

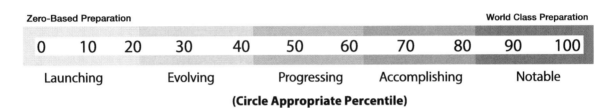

Zero-Based Preparation   World Class Preparation

| 0 | 10 | 20 | 30 | 40 | 50 | 60 | 70 | 80 | 90 | 100 |

Launching   Evolving   Progressing   Accomplishing   Notable

(Circle Appropriate Percentile)

Zero-Based Organization	World-Class Organization
• Organization's work systems are not formalized and do not capitalize on diverse thinking among employees regarding identification of innovative opportunities and ideas that promote high performance work. • Organization's work systems do not support employee interaction that address innovative workforce issues and opportunities from diverse ideas, cultures, and thinking.	• Organization's work teams, process teams, and peer coaching teams encourage high performance and promote diverse ideas and thinking throughout the organization about corporate innovation opportunities, issues, and vulnerabilities. • Organization promotes cross-functional teams among employees to capitalize on their diverse ideas, cultures, and diverse thinking to identify innovative opportunities, issues and vulnerabilities.

☐ Approach   ☐ Deployment   ☐ Learning   ☐ Integration

5.1a(2)   The organization's culture promotes open communication, high performance work, and an engaged workforce that benefits from diverse ideas, cultures, and thinking as they relate to corporate innovation.

+ Strengths

1.

2.

3.

- Opportunities for Improvement

1.

2.

3.

Corporate Innovation Planning Issues:

Short Term (1 to 2 years)

1.

2.

Long Term (2 years or more)

1.

2.

5.1a(3)   How does your organization's workforce performance management system support corporate innovation initiatives within the organization and reward, recognize, and compensate the workforce for reinforcing a customer and business focus and achievement of your action plans?

Interview notes:

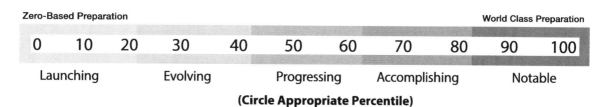

Zero-Based Preparation   World Class Preparation

| 0 | 10 | 20 | 30 | 40 | 50 | 60 | 70 | 80 | 90 | 100 |

Launching   Evolving   Progressing   Accomplishing   Notable

(Circle Appropriate Percentile)

Zero-Based Organization	World-Class Organization
• Organization's performance management system does not support or promote addressing corporate innovation issues among employees. • Organization allows only senior management to be involved with corporate innovation initiatives.	• Organization groups employees into cross-functional teams. Each team collects data that may be used to gauge performance results of corporate innovation initiatives. • Organization's performance management system supports and recognizes employee involvement and support for its corporate innovation efforts and rewards and compensates employees who focus on innovative solutions and achievement of action plans.

☐ Approach ☐ Deployment ☐ Learning ☐ Integration

5.1a (3)   The organization's workforce performance management system supports corporate innovation initiatives within the organization and rewards, recognizes, and compensates the workforce for reinforcing a customer and business focus and achievement of action plans.

+ Strengths
1.
2.
3.

- Opportunities for Improvement
1.
2.
3.

Corporate Innovation Planning Issues:

Short Term (1 to 2 years)
1.
2.

Long Term (2 years or more)
1.
2.

5.1b(1)   How does your organization's learning and development system address core competencies, strategic challenges, accomplishment of its action plans, performance improvement, ethics, training, coaching, mentoring and work-related experiences as they relate to corporate innovation?

Interview notes:

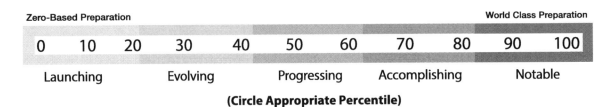

(Circle Appropriate Percentile)

Zero-Based Organization	World-Class Organization
• Organization's education and training offerings do not support corporate innovation strategic goals. • Organization has limited in-house training/development that contributes to the accomplishment of strategic challenges, ethics, innovation, and performance improvement action plans. Most training and leadership development initiatives related to corporate innovation are contracted through outside training/consulting groups.	• Organization's employee training and development needs are integrated with its short and long-term strategic plans and goals that support corporate innovation. • Organization's employee workshops and training programs address topics that support and are aligned with the company's corporate innovation goals and action plans.

☐ Approach   ☐ Deployment   ☐ Learning   ☐ Integration

5.1b (1)   The organization's learning and development system addresses core competencies, strategic challenges, accomplishment of its action plans, performance improvement, ethics, training, coaching, mentoring and work-related experiences as they relate to corporate innovation.

+ Strengths
1.
2.
3.

- Opportunities for Improvement
1.
2.
3.

Corporate Innovation Planning Issues:

Short Term (1 to 2 years)
1.
2.

Long Term (2 years or more)
1.
2.

5.1b(2)   How does your organization's workforce learning and development system address transfer of knowledge from departing or retiring workers and reinforce new knowledge and skills on the job as they relate to corporate innovation?

Interview notes:

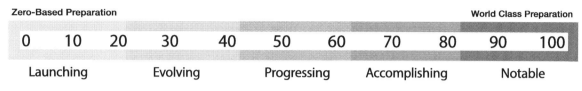

Zero-Based Preparation   World Class Preparation

| 0 | 10 | 20 | 30 | 40 | 50 | 60 | 70 | 80 | 90 | 100 |

Launching   Evolving   Progressing   Accomplishing   Notable

(Circle Appropriate Percentile)

Zero-Based Organization	World-Class Organization
• Organization has no process in place to ensure that knowledge and skills received by employees in training/development sessions conducted through Corporate Innovation has on-the-job application and that all transfer knowledge related to corporate innovation is being protected. • Organization is not concerned about capturing, and protecting knowledge and intellectual capital from departing or retiring workers and ensuring that all corporate innovation knowledge is not being transferred to competitive organizations.	• Organization has an evaluation process in place to ensure that new knowledge received by employees in training sessions has on-the-job application and that all corporate innovation knowledge is protected and is secure. • Senior leadership recognizes employees who apply innovative knowledge and skills received through Corporate Innovation, and who protect the organization's intellectual capital by ensuring that corporate intelligence and innovative practices are being protected when transferring that knowledge to co-workers.

☐ Approach   ☐ Deployment   ☐ Learning   ☐ Integration

5.1b(2)   The organization's workforce learning and development system addresses transfer of knowledge from departing or retiring workers and reinforces new knowledge and skills on the job as they relate to corporate innovation.

+ Strengths
1.
2.
3.

- Opportunities for Improvement
1.
2.
3.

Corporate Innovation Planning Issues:

Short Term (1 to 2 years)
1.
2.

Long Term (2 years of more)
1.
2.

5.1b (3)   How does your organization evaluate the effectiveness and efficiency of its learning and development systems and ensure consistency as they relate to corporate innovation?

Interview notes:

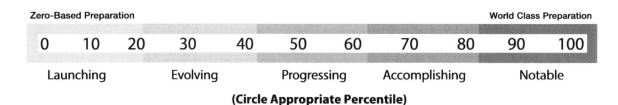

Zero-Based Preparation										World Class Preparation
0	10	20	30	40	50	60	70	80	90	100
Launching		Evolving		Progressing		Accomplishing			Notable	

(Circle Appropriate Percentile)

Zero-Based Organization	World-Class Organization
• Organization has no process in place to review its education and training effectiveness and efficiency as it relates to corporate innovation. • Organization does not evaluate the effectiveness and efficiency of their learning and development systems and uses only anecdotal information to gauge its impact on promoting corporate innovation.	• Organization has a formal evaluation process for all training and education that is delivered. Each training session promotes corporate innovation and receives participant evaluation. These findings are used for curriculum improvement. • Organization evaluates on-the-job application of corporate innovation for all training and education delivered to employees. A team reviews all input to improve education, training curriculum and increased application of corporate innovation within the various corporate projects being conducted corporate-wide.

☐ Approach   ☐ Deployment   ☐ Learning   ☐ Integration

5.1b (3)   The organization evaluates the effectiveness and efficiency of its learning and development systems and ensures consistency as they relate to corporate innovation.

+ Strengths
1.
2.
3.

- Opportunities for Improvement
1.
2.
3.

Corporate Innovation Planning Issues:
    Short Term (1 to 2 years)
    1.
    2.

    Long Term (2 years or more)
    1.
    2.

5.1b(4)   How does your organization manage effective career progression and accomplish effective succession planning for management and leadership positions as they relate to corporate innovation?

Interview notes:

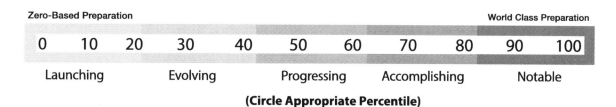

(Circle Appropriate Percentile)

Zero-Based Organization	World-Class Organization
• Organization has no processes in place to motivate employees to develop and use their full potential to ensure a sustainable work environment that promotes corporate innovation. • Organization has no concern for motivating employees to develop their knowledge and skills through a formal succession planning process that will ensure a sustainable and innovative work environment.	• Organization has developed a leadership academy to motivate employees to attain job- and career-related development and to use their full potential to ensure that future managers and leaders are devoted to promoting corporate innovation. • Organization has a formal recognition program in place that motivates and rewards employees to develop and use their full potential in ensuring a sustainable work environment that promotes on-going succession planning within an innovative environment.

☐ Approach   ☐ Deployment   ☐ Learning   ☐ Integration

5.1b(4)   The organization manages effective career progression and accomplishes effective succession planning for management and leadership positions as they relate to corporate innovation.

+ Strengths
1.
2.
3.

- Opportunities for Improvement
1.
2.
3.

Corporate Innovation Planning Issues:
Short Term (1 to 2 years)
1.
2.

Long Term (2 years or more)
1.
2.

5.1c (1)   How does your organization assess workforce engagement as it relates to corporate innovation?

Interview notes:

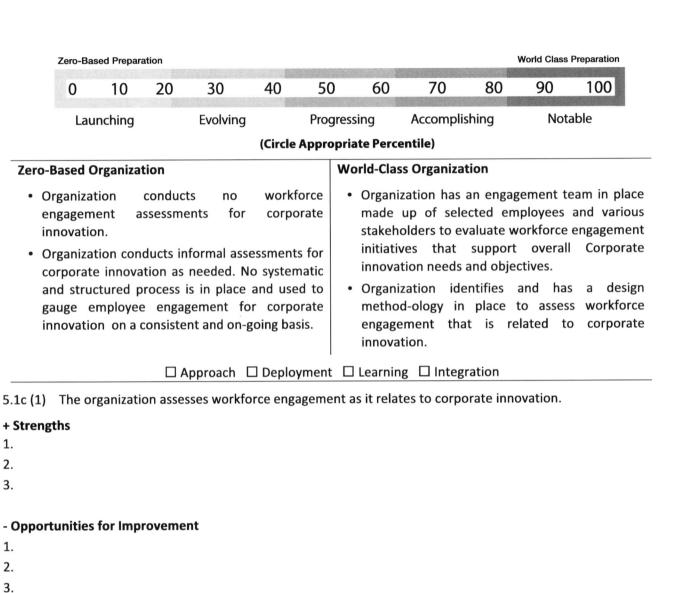

Zero-Based Preparation   **World Class Preparation**

| 0 | 10 | 20 | 30 | 40 | 50 | 60 | 70 | 80 | 90 | 100 |

Launching   Evolving   Progressing   Accomplishing   Notable

(Circle Appropriate Percentile)

Zero-Based Organization	World-Class Organization
• Organization conducts no workforce engagement assessments for corporate innovation. • Organization conducts informal assessments for corporate innovation as needed. No systematic and structured process is in place and used to gauge employee engagement for corporate innovation on a consistent and on-going basis.	• Organization has an engagement team in place made up of selected employees and various stakeholders to evaluate workforce engagement initiatives that support overall Corporate innovation needs and objectives. • Organization identifies and has a design method-ology in place to assess workforce engagement that is related to corporate innovation.

☐ Approach ☐ Deployment ☐ Learning ☐ Integration

5.1c (1)   The organization assesses workforce engagement as it relates to corporate innovation.

+ Strengths
1.
2.
3.

- Opportunities for Improvement
1.
2.
3.

Corporate Innovation Planning Issues:

Short Term (1 to 2 years)
1.
2.

Long Term (2 years or more)
1.
2.

5.1c (2)   How does your organization relate workforce engagement assessment findings to key business results as they relate to corporate innovation?

Interview notes:

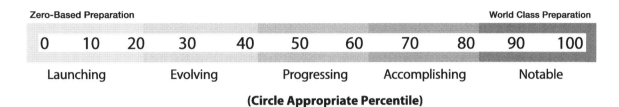

(Circle Appropriate Percentile)

Zero-Based Organization	World-Class Organization
• Organization has nothing in place that addresses workforce engagement issues and their impact on corporate innovation. • Organization does not relate workplace safety and security, diversity, and teamwork to workforce engagement and corporate innovation results.	• Organization assesses and aligns their workforce grievance resolution, career development, safety and security, and teamwork initiatives with their corporate innovation business results on an annual basis. • Organization uses formal surveys and focus group data and information to assess turnover, grievances, and employee recognition results as they relate to corporate innovation.

☐ Approach   ☐ Deployment   ☐ Learning   ☐ Integration

5.1c (2)   The organization relates workforce engagement assessment findings to key business results as they relate to corporate innovation.

+ Strengths
1.
2.
3.

- Opportunities for Improvement
1.
2.
3.

Corporate Innovation Planning Issues:

Short Term (1 to 2 years)
1.
2.

Long Term (2 years or more)
1.
2.

5.2   Workforce Environment (40 pts.)

Describe how your organization manages workforce capability and capacity to accomplish the work of the organization as it promotes corporate innovation. Describe how your organization maintains a safe, secure, supportive, and innovative work climate.

QUESTIONS TO ADDRESS

5.2a (1)   How does your organization assess your workforce capability and capacity needs, including skills, competencies, and staffing levels that promotes corporate innovation?

5.2a (2)   How does your organization recruit, hire, place, and retain new members of the workforce that promotes corporate innovation?

5.2a (3)   How does your organization manage and organize a workforce that promotes corporate innovation?

5.2a (4)   How does your organization prepare the workforce for changing capability and capacity needs and maintain an environment that promotes corporate innovation?

5.2b (1)   How does your organization address workplace environmental factors to ensure and improve workforce health, safety, and security through corporate innovation?

5.2b (2)   How does your organization support a workforce via policies, services, and benefits through corporate innovation?

5.2 Percent Score

☑ Approach   ☑ Deployment   ☑ Learning   ☑ Integration

5.2a (1)   How does your organization assess your workforce capability and capacity needs, including skills, competencies, and staffing levels that promotes corporate innovation?

Interview notes:

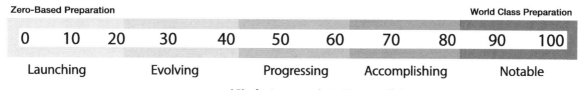

Zero-Based Preparation   World Class Preparation

| 0 | 10 | 20 | 30 | 40 | 50 | 60 | 70 | 80 | 90 | 100 |

Launching   Evolving   Progressing   Accomplishing   Notable

(Circle Appropriate Percentile)

Zero-Based Organization	World-Class Organization
• No systematic process is in place to assess work and jobs for employees that promote cooperation, empowerment, innovation, and collaboration. • Organization does not address work system structure that promotes cooperation and collaboration of employees that promote corporate innovation.	• Organization conducts an annual work system review to ensure that employees' cooperation and collaboration on innovative corporate projects meet the capability and capacity needs and goals. • Employees are grouped into various corporate innovation work teams (e.g. cross-functional teams) to promote cooperation and collaboration and to keep current capability and capacity staffing needs. Corporate innovation work teams ensure that workforce skills and competencies are adequate for the organization to meet its strategic goals and plans.

☐ Approach   ☐ Deployment   ☐ Learning   ☐ Integration

5.2a(1)   The organization assesses workforce capability and capacity needs, including skills, competencies, and staffing levels that promotes corporate innovation.

+ Strengths
1.
2.
3.

- Opportunities for Improvement
1.
2.
3.

Corporate Innovation Planning Issues:

   Short Term (1 to 2 years)
   1.
   2.

   Long Term (2 years or more)
   1.
   2.

5.2a (2)   How does your organization recruit, hire, place, and retain new members of the workforce that promotes corporate innovation?

Interview notes:

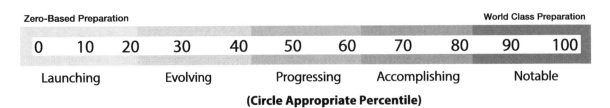

Zero-Based Preparation   World Class Preparation

| 0 | 10 | 20 | 30 | 40 | 50 | 60 | 70 | 80 | 90 | 100 |

Launching   Evolving   Progressing   Accomplishing   Notable

(Circle Appropriate Percentile)

Zero-Based Organization	World-Class Organization
• Organization has no consistent corporate innovation policies or procedures that address recruiting, hiring, and retaining new employees. • Organization has not established a consistent policy for recruitment, hiring, placing, and retention for potential and newly hired employees that promote corporate innovation.	• Organization has documented procedures in place that address recruiting, hiring, and retaining new employees that promote corporate innovation. • Organization has developed a formal orientation program for potential and newly hired employees that promotes the Corporate Vision, Mission, and Values and innovation goals and plans.

☐ Approach   ☐ Deployment   ☐ Learning   ☐ Integration

5.2a (2)   The organization recruits, hires, places, and retains new members of the workforce that promotes corporate innovation.

+ Strengths

1.

2.

3.

- Opportunities for Improvement

1.

2.

3.

Corporate Innovation Planning Issues:

Short Term (1 to 2 years)

1.

2.

Long Term (2 years or more)

1.

2.

5.2a (3)   How does your organization manage and organize a workforce that promotes corporate innovation?

Interview notes:

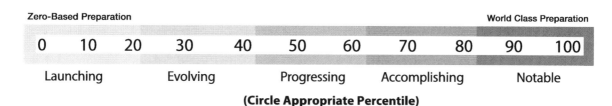

(Circle Appropriate Percentile)

Zero-Based Organization	World-Class Organization
• Organization has no process in place to ensure effective communication, cooperation, and knowledge/skill sharing among employees that promotes corporate innovation. • Organization does not have a formal structure in place to manage and organize the workforce that promotes corporate innovation.	• Organization has in place cross-functional teams to share their corporate project results in the organization's password protected intranet. This ensures more effective communication among teams throughout the workforce and encourages all employees to better understand each team's project results and to promote corporate innovation. • Organization manages all work projects through cross-functional teams that are recognized for innovative projects and rewarded for results.

☐ Approach   ☐ Deployment   ☐ Learning   ☐ Integration

5.2a (3)   The organization manages and organizes a workforce that promotes corporate innovation.

+ Strengths
1.
2.
3.

- Opportunities for Improvement
1.
2.
3.

Corporate Innovation Planning Issues:

Short Term (1 to 2 years)
1.
2.

Long Term (2 years or more)
1.
2.

5.2a (4)   How does your organization prepare the workforce for changing capability and capacity needs and maintain an environment that promotes corporate innovation.?

Interview notes:

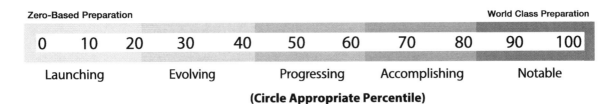

(Circle Appropriate Percentile)

Zero-Based Organization	World-Class Organization
• Organization has nothing in place to ensure that workforce capability and capacity needs are being addressed throughout the organization and that corporate innovation is being maintained.	• Organization has formal plans in place to notify employees in advance of any potential workforce reductions to meet seasonal or varying demand levels and to ensure that corporate innovation is being promoted.
• Organization has no well-defined process in place to prepare the workforce for capability changes such as technology enhancements, and capacity changes needed to ensure sufficient staffing levels are in place to maintain a consistent operation that promotes corporate innovation.	• Organization uses forecast reports to anticipate changing capability and capacity workforce changes based on varying customer demand levels to ensure that any workforce disruption and corporate innovation are being addressed and that staffing levels and the promotion of innovative practices are being protected during all workforce changes. The forecast information is shared on a monthly basis with all management levels.

☐ Approach ☐ Deployment ☐ Learning ☐ Integration

5.2a (4)   The organization prepares the workforce for changing capability and capacity needs and maintains an environment that promotes corporate innovation.

+ Strengths
1.
2.
3.

- Opportunities for Improvement
1.
2.
3.

Corporate Innovation Planning Issues:

Short Term (1 to 2 years)
1.
2.

Long Term (2 years or more)
1.
2.

5.2b (1)   How does your organization address workplace environmental factors to ensure and improve workforce health, safety, and security through corporate innovation?

Interview notes:

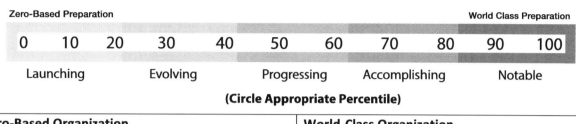

(Circle Appropriate Percentile)

Zero-Based Organization	World-Class Organization
• Organization does not address workplace environmental factors to ensure that workforce health, safety, and security throughout the workforce is improving through corporate innovation. • Organization has no concern for workforce environmental factors that ensure and improve health, safety, and security of the workforce through corporate innovation.	• Organization has in place strategic plans and goals that address workforce health, safety, and security issues through corporate innovation practices. • Organization has training, education, and monthly employee meetings that address workplace health, safety, and security issues/concerns through corporate innovation practices.

☐ Approach   ☐ Deployment   ☐ Learning   ☐ Integration

5.2b (1)   The organization addresses workplace environmental factors to ensure and improve workforce health, safety, and security through corporate innovation.

+ Strengths

1.

2.

3.

- Opportunities for Improvement

1.

2.

3.

Corporate Innovation Planning Issues:

Short Term (1 to 2 years)

1.

2.

Long Term (2 years or more)

1.

2.

5.2b (2)   How does your organization support a workforce via policies, services, and benefits through corporate innovation?

Interview notes:

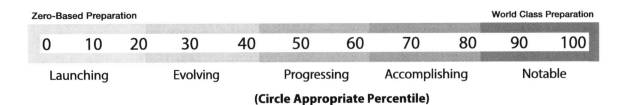

Launching   Evolving   Progressing   Accomplishing   Notable

(Circle Appropriate Percentile)

Zero-Based Organization	World-Class Organization
• Organization does nothing to maintain a safe, secure, and healthful work environment that supports and protects the workforce through corporate innovation. • Organization's leadership has no concern for maintaining an environment that is safe, secure, and healthful and one that supports the well-being, satisfaction, and motivation of employees through policies, services, and benefits that promote corporate innovation.	• Organization surveys employees to determine to what extent the work environment supports their physical and mental well-being and innovative thinking. Findings are used to address areas of concern within the workforce and to ensure that corporate innovation is being promoted. • Organization provides counseling to employees regarding issues that are related to dissatisfaction within their work environment. Policies, services, and benefits have been developed to support and to protect the workforce through innovative practices.

☐ Approach   ☐ Deployment   ☐ Learning   ☐ Integration

5.2b (2)   The organization supports a workforce via policies, services, and benefits through corporate innovation.

+ Strengths

1.

2.

3.

- Opportunities for Improvement

1.

2.

3.

Corporate Innovation Planning Issues:

Short Term (1 to 2 years)

1.

2.

Long Term (2 years or more)

1.

2.

8 Category 6 Process Management

6 Process Management (85 pts.) [29]

The Process Management Category examines how your organization designs its work systems and how it designs, manages, improves, and secures its key processes for implementing those work systems throughout the organization to deliver customer value and achieve organizational success through corporate innovation. Also examined is your readiness for emergencies.

6.1   Work Systems   (35 pts.)

Describe how your organization designs its work systems and determines its key processes to deliver customer value through corporate innovation, prepare for potential emergencies, achieve organizational success.

QUESTIONS TO ADDRESS

6.1a (1)   How does your organization design and innovate overall work systems?

6.1a (2)   How do your organization's work systems and key work processes enhance core competencies and reduce variability through corporate innovation?

6.1b (1)   What are your organization's key work processes that are enhanced through corporate innovation?

6.1b (2)   How does your organization determine key work process requirements through corporate innovation utilizing input from customers, venders, partners, and collaborators?

6.1c   How does your organization ensure work systems and workplace preparedness for disasters or emergencies that protect the safety and security of the workforce through corporate innovation?

☐   **6.1 Percent Score**

☑Approach   ☑Deployment   ☑Learning   ☑Integration

6.1a (1)   How does your organization design and innovate overall work systems?

Interview notes:

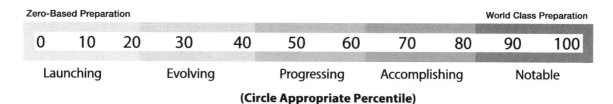

(Circle Appropriate Percentile)

Zero-Based Organization	World-Class Organization
• Organization has no concern for key process designs and innovative work systems. Most process designs are completed just-in-time for service delivery and innovation is never considered in the design process.	• Organization conducts assessments to ensure that critical work processes meet design requirements and incorporate cycle time and other efficiency and effectiveness factors through innovative procedures.
• Organization does not have a formal design process in place for their work systems. All work system designs are done prior to service delivery and on an informal random basis.	• Organization's designs are reviewed by cross-functional employee and stakeholder teams to ensure that innovative design requirements are being met and are protected from competitors.

☐ Approach   ☐ Deployment   ☐ Learning   ☐ Integration

6.1a (1)   The organization designs and innovates overall work systems.

+ Strengths

1.

2.

3.

- Opportunities for Improvement

1.

2.

3.

Corporate Innovation Planning Issues:

Short Term (1 to 2 years)

1.

2.

Long Term (2 years or more)

1.

2.

6.1a (2)   How do your organization's work systems and key work processes enhance core competencies and reduce variability through corporate innovation?

Interview notes:

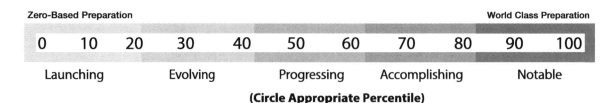

| Launching | Evolving | Progressing | Accomplishing | Notable |

(Circle Appropriate Percentile)

Zero-Based Organization	World-Class Organization
• Organization has no design of new programs and services based on the organization's work systems and key work processes. • Organization has no process in place for program and service designs. New programs and service offerings that are designed internally and reflect stakeholder input and focus on value-creation processes for customers do not exist.	• Processes are identified and flowcharted and designed to address the most critical work system requirements. These processes are considered the organization's core competencies and are reviewed quarterly to ensure that all work systems and key work processes are innovative and efficient. Processes are designed to reduce variability. • Employees at all levels are updated and asked to review all new initiatives (Programs/Services) to ensure that they are innovative. New initiatives must meet key design requirements, focus on key value-added creation processes, enhance core competencies, and reduce variability.

☐ Approach   ☐ Deployment   ☐ Learning   ☐ Integration

6.1a (2)   The organization's work systems and key work processes enhance core competencies and reduce variability through corporate innovation.

+ Strengths

1.

2.

3.

- Opportunities for Improvement

1.

2.

3.

Corporate Innovation Planning Issues:

Short Term (1 to 2 years)

   1.

   2.

Long Term (2 years or more)

   1.

   2.

6.1b (1)   What are your organization's key work processes that are enhanced through corporate innovation?

Interview notes:

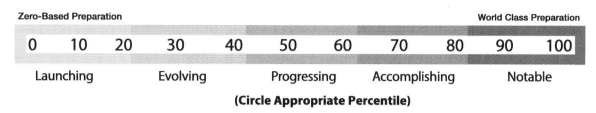

(Circle Appropriate Percentile)

Zero-Based Organization	World-Class Organization
• Organization has not identified its key work processes and is not concerned with innovative enhancements. • Organization determines key work processes that need to be flowcharted and reviewed for process efficiency without input from employee and stakeholder groups and with no concern for corporate innovation enhancements.	• Organization determines its key work processes that need to be flowcharted and reviewed for process efficiency and innovative practices based on focus group input from key stakeholder groups. • Organization annually surveys employees, vendors, customers, and partners to determine key work processes and practices that need to be reviewed for efficiency, consistency, and innovation in service delivery.

☐ Approach   ☐ Deployment   ☐ Learning   ☐ Integration

6.1b (1)   The organization's key work processes are enhanced through corporate innovation.

+ Strengths

1.

2.

3.

- Opportunities for Improvement

1.

2.

3.

Corporate Innovation Planning Issues:

Short Term (1 to 2 years)

1.

2.

Long Term (2 years or more)

1.

2.

6.1b (2)   How does your organization determine key work process requirements through corporate innovation utilizing input from customers, suppliers, partners, and collaborators?

Interview notes:

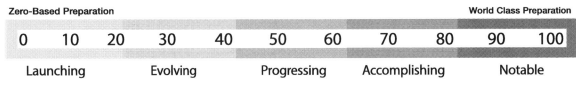

Zero-Based Preparation / World Class Preparation

0   10   20   30   40   50   60   70   80   90   100

Launching   Evolving   Progressing   Accomplishing   Notable

(Circle Appropriate Percentile)

Zero-Based Organization	World-Class Organization
• Organization does not use a systematic approach to evaluate and improve key value creation processes, nor is there any concern among senior staff to determine key work process requirements through corporate innovation. • Organization does not include stakeholders to help determine key work process requirements through corporate innovation, and does not seek, nor value any input they may offer for process improvements.	• Organization has a structured evaluation process to ensure that key process requirements are identified and flowcharted and involve all stakeholder groups. All intellectual capital is being identified and cataloged to ensure on-going innovative practices. • Organization incorporates simple flowcharting of key work processes and solicits input from employees, customers, suppliers, partners, and collaborators for innovative idea sharing.

☐ Approach   ☐ Deployment   ☐ Learning   ☐ Integration

6.1b (2)   The organization determines key work process requirements through corporate innovation utilizing input from customers, vendors, partners, and collaborators.

+ Strengths

1.

2.

3.

- Opportunities for Improvement

1.

2.

3.

Corporate Innovation Planning Issues:

Short Term (1 to 2 years)

1.

2.

Long Term (2 years or more)

1.

2.

6.1c   How does your organization ensure work systems and workplace preparedness for disasters or emergencies that protect the safety and security of the workforce through corporate innovation?

Interview notes:

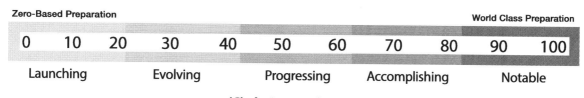

Zero-Based Preparation   **World Class Preparation**

| 0 | 10 | 20 | 30 | 40 | 50 | 60 | 70 | 80 | 90 | 100 |

Launching   Evolving   Progressing   Accomplishing   Notable

(Circle Appropriate Percentile)

Zero-Based Organization	**World-Class Organization**
• Organization has no Business Continuity Plan in place that addresses workplace preparedness for disasters and/or emergencies that will ensure ongoing protection of the workforce. • Organization has not formally addressed emergency planning for weather-related, utility-related, security-related local or national disasters, including potential pandemics..	• Organization has a formal Business Continuity Plan in place that addresses key work systems and innovative workplace preparedness issues. • Organization has conducted a series of mock disaster drills; throughout the workforce, to ensure that innovative work system and workplace preparedness initiatives are in place to maintain continuous service delivery in the midst of disasters and/or emergencies..

☐ Approach   ☐ Deployment   ☐ Learning   ☐ Integration

6.1c   The organization ensures work system and workplace preparedness for disasters or emergencies that protect the safety and security of the workforce through corporate innovation.

+ Strengths

1.

2.

3.

- Opportunities for Improvement

1.

2.

3.

Corporate Innovation Planning Issues:

   Short Term (1 to 2 years)

   1.

   2.

   Long Term (2 years or more)

   1.

   2.

6.2   Work Processes   (50 pts.)

Describe how your organization designs, implements, manages, and improves its key work processes to deliver customer value and achieve organizational success through corporate innovation.

QUESTIONS TO ADDRESS

6.2a   How does your organization design and innovate your work processes to meet all key corporate requirements?

6.2b (1) How does your organization implement, manage, and innovate work processes to ensure that they meet design requirements?

6.2b(2) How does your organization control and minimize the overall costs of inspections, tests, and process or performance audits for key work processes through corporate innovation?

6.2c   How does your organization improve work processes to achieve better performance, reduce variability, improve products/services, and keep those processes current with business needs and directions through innovative practices?

6.2 Percent Score

☑Approach   ☑Deployment   ☑Learning   ☑Integration

6.2a   How does your organization design and innovate your work processes to meet all key corporate requirements?

Interview notes:

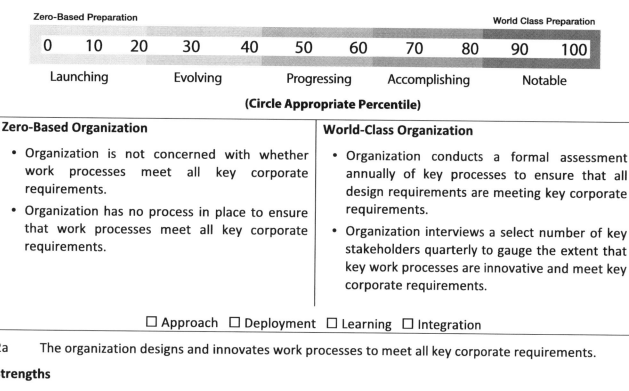

Zero-Based Preparation   World Class Preparation

| 0 | 10 | 20 | 30 | 40 | 50 | 60 | 70 | 80 | 90 | 100 |

Launching   Evolving   Progressing   Accomplishing   Notable

(Circle Appropriate Percentile)

Zero-Based Organization	World-Class Organization
• Organization is not concerned with whether work processes meet all key corporate requirements. • Organization has no process in place to ensure that work processes meet all key corporate requirements.	• Organization conducts a formal assessment annually of key processes to ensure that all design requirements are meeting key corporate requirements. • Organization interviews a select number of key stakeholders quarterly to gauge the extent that key work processes are innovative and meet key corporate requirements.

□ Approach   □ Deployment   □ Learning   □ Integration

6.2a   The organization designs and innovates work processes to meet all key corporate requirements.

+ Strengths
1.
2.
3.

- Opportunities for Improvement
1.
2.
3.

Corporate Innovation Planning Issues:

Short Term (1 to 2 years)
1.
2.

Long Term (2 years or more)
1.
2.

6.2b (1)   How does your organization implement, manage, and innovate work processes to ensure that they meet design requirements?

Interview notes:

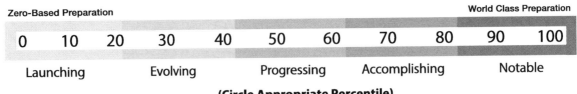

Zero-Based Preparation				World Class Preparation
0 10 20	30 40	50 60	70 80	90 100
Launching	Evolving	Progressing	Accomplishing	Notable

(Circle Appropriate Percentile)

Zero-Based Organization	**World-Class Organization**
• Organization does not have a systematic approach to evaluate and improve key design processes that meet customer requirements.	• Organization has a structured evaluation process in place to ensure that all key processes are innovative, meet design requirements, achieve better performance, reduce variability, and improved effectiveness.
• Organization does not evaluate its work processes to ensure that innovation, better performance, reduced variability, and improved effectiveness are addressed in the design requirements.	• Organization conducts pilot tests on all key customer processes to ensure that innovation, better performance, reduced variability, and improved effectiveness are being addressed in the design requirements.

☐ Approach   ☐ Deployment   ☐ Learning   ☐ Integration

6.2b (1)   The organization implements, manages, and innovates work processes to ensure that they meet design requirements.

+ Strengths

1.

2.

3.

- Opportunities for Improvement

1.

2.

3.

Corporate Innovation Planning Issues:

Short Term (1 to 2 years)

   1.

   2.

Long Term (2 years or more)

   1.

   2.

6.2b(2)   How does your organization control and minimize the overall costs of inspections, tests, and process or performance audits for key work processes through corporate innovation?

Interview notes:

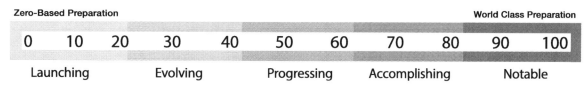

Zero-Based Preparation   **World Class Preparation**

| 0 | 10 | 20 | 30 | 40 | 50 | 60 | 70 | 80 | 90 | 100 |

Launching   Evolving   Progressing   Accomplishing   Notable

(Circle Appropriate Percentile)

Zero-Based Organization	**World-Class Organization**
• Organization has no process in place to minimize overall costs associated with inspections, tests, and process or performance audits. • Organization occasionally uses in-house self-assessment teams to conduct audits and to minimize costs. Organization rarely considers reviewing performance issues that relate to the audits.	• Organization uses in-house cross-functional employee teams to review innovative practices, conduct inspections, tests, and process audits to minimize overall costs. • Organization minimizes overall costs associated with conducting process and performance audits by conducting a self-assessment via in-house stakeholder teams.

☐ Approach   ☐ Deployment   ☐ Learning   ☐ Integration

6.2b(2)   The organization controls and minimizes the overall costs of inspections, tests, and process or performance audits for key work processes through corporate innovation.

+ Strengths

1.

2.

3.

- Opportunities for Improvement

1.

2.

3.

Corporate Innovation Planning Issues:

Short Term (1 to 2 years)

1.

2.

Long Term (2 years or more)

1.

2.

6.2c   How does your organization improve work processes to achieve better performance, reduce variability, improve products/services and keep those processes current with business needs and directions through innovative practices?

Interview notes:

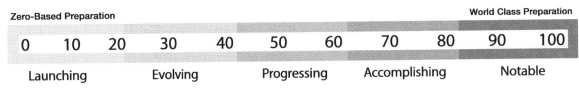

Zero-Based Preparation   World Class Preparation

| 0 | 10 | 20 | 30 | 40 | 50 | 60 | 70 | 80 | 90 | 100 |

Launching   Evolving   Progressing   Accomplishing   Notable

(Circle Appropriate Percentile)

Zero-Based Organization	**World-Class Organization**
• Organization has no key performance measures or indicators to control and/or improve key processes and practices. • Organization does not compare or benchmark other organizations' key performance measures or indicators to ensure that best practice and innovative processes/practices are in place.	• Organization has developed a process scoreboard to control and improve key processes and to keep innovative practices current with business needs and directions. • Organization conducts biannual assessments to measure the extent key processes are in control against the design of the process. Findings are used to improve each key process and to ensure that innovative processes/practices are current and up-to-date.

☐ Approach   ☐ Deployment   ☐ Learning   ☐ Integration

6.2c   The organization improves work processes to achieve better performance, reduce variability, improve products/services and keeps those processes current with business needs and directions through innovative practices.

+ Strengths

1.

2.

3.

- Opportunities for Improvement

1.

2.

3.

Corporate Innovation Planning Issues:

Short Term (1 to 2 years)

1.

2.

Long Term (2 years or more)

1.

2.

9 Category 7 Results

7 Results (450 pts.) [30]

The Results Category examines your organization's performance and improvement in key innovative product/service areas – program/service outcomes, customer-focused outcomes, financial and market outcomes, workforce-focused outcomes, process effectiveness outcomes, and leadership outcomes. Performance levels are examined relative to those of competitors and other organizations with similar innovative product/service offerings that are known for their notable results.

7.1   Product/Service Outcomes   (100 pts.)

Summarize your organization's key performance results for innovative products/services.   Segment your results by product/service offerings, customer groups, and market segments, as appropriate.   Include appropriate comparative data.

RESULTS

QUESTIONS TO ADDRESS

7.1a   What are your organization's current levels and trends of innovative product/service performance that are considered important to customers?

7.1 Percent Score

Performance Levels   Trends   Comparisons   Linkage   Gap

7.1a   What are your organization's current levels and trends of innovative product/service performance that are considered important to customers?

Interview notes:

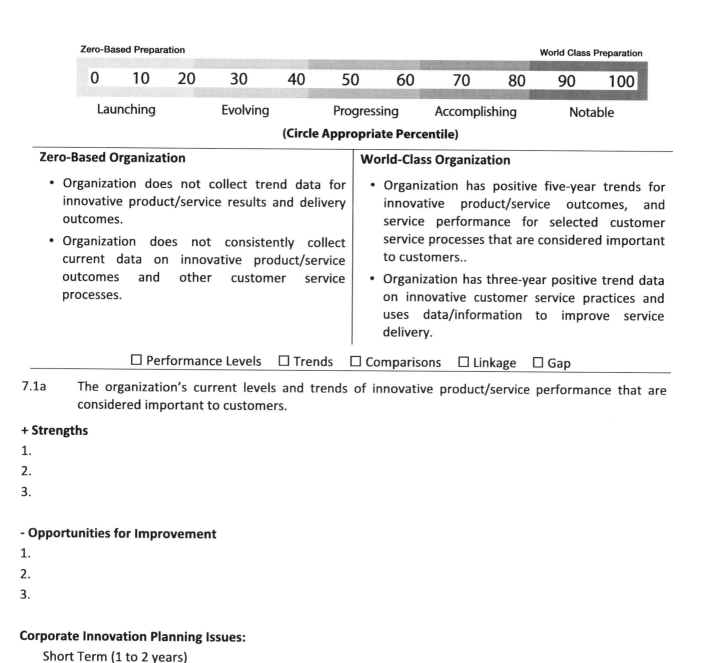

Zero-Based Preparation   **World Class Preparation**

0   10   20   30   40   50   60   70   80   90   100

Launching   Evolving   Progressing   Accomplishing   Notable

(Circle Appropriate Percentile)

Zero-Based Organization	**World-Class Organization**
• Organization does not collect trend data for innovative product/service results and delivery outcomes. • Organization does not consistently collect current data on innovative product/service outcomes and other customer service processes.	• Organization has positive five-year trends for innovative product/service outcomes, and service performance for selected customer service processes that are considered important to customers.. • Organization has three-year positive trend data on innovative customer service practices and uses data/information to improve service delivery.

☐ Performance Levels   ☐ Trends   ☐ Comparisons   ☐ Linkage   ☐ Gap

7.1a   The organization's current levels and trends of innovative product/service performance that are considered important to customers.

+ Strengths

1.

2.

3.

- Opportunities for Improvement

1.

2.

3.

Corporate Innovation Planning Issues:

Short Term (1 to 2 years)

1.

2.

Long Term (2 years or more)

1.

2.

7.2   Customer Focused Outcomes   (70 pts.)

Summarize your organization's key customer- focused results for customer satisfaction, dissatisfaction, and engagement regarding innovative products/services. Segment your results by offerings, customer groups, and market segments, as appropriate. Include appropriate comparative data.

RESULTS

QUESTIONS TO ADDRESS

7.2a(1)   What are your organization's current levels and trends of customer satisfaction and dissatisfaction with your organization's innovative product/service offerings?

7.2a(2)   What are your organization's current levels and trends of customer relationship building and engagement as they relate to innovative products/services?

7.2 Percent Score

☑ **Performance Levels**   ☑ **Trends**   ☑ **Comparisons**   ☑ **Linkage**   ☑ **Gap**

7.2a(1) What are your organization's current levels and trends of customer satisfaction and dissatisfaction with your organization's innovative product/service offerings?

Interview notes:

Zero-Based Preparation									World Class Preparation	
0	10	20	30	40	50	60	70	80	90	100
Launching		Evolving			Progressing		Accomplishing		Notable	

(Circle Appropriate Percentile)

Zero-Based Organization	World-Class Organization
• Organization does not trend satisfaction and dissatisfaction data to gauge customer concerns regarding the organization's innovative product/ service offerings. • Organization does not collect satisfaction/ dissatisfaction data from customers to gauge product/service satisfaction.	• Organization collects and trends satisfaction and dissatisfaction data to gauge customers' ongoing satisfaction with their key innovative product/service offerings. • Organization uses customer satisfaction/ dissatisfaction trend data to improve its present innovative product/service offerings and to identify market trends for future innovative offerings.

☐ Performance Levels   ☐ Trends   ☐ Comparisons   ☐ Linkage   ☐ Gap

7.2a(1) The organization's current levels and trends of customer satisfaction and dissatisfaction with your organization's innovative product/service offerings.

+ Strengths
1.
2.
3.

- Opportunities for Improvement
1.
2.
3.

Corporate Innovation Planning Issues:
   Short Term (1 to 2 years)
   1.
   2.

   Long Term (2 years or more)
   1.
   2.

7.2a(2) What are your organization's current levels and trends of customer relationship building and engagement as they relate to innovative products/services?

Interview notes:

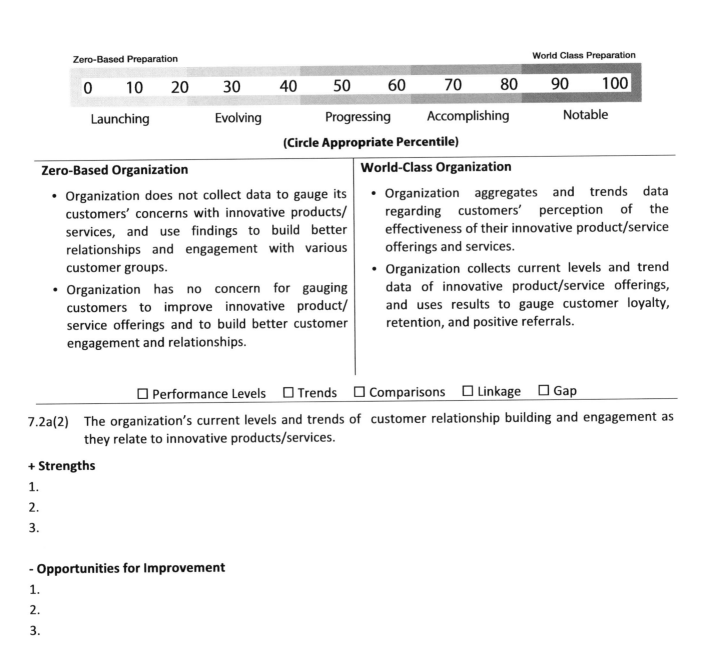

Zero-Based Preparation   World Class Preparation

| 0 | 10 | 20 | 30 | 40 | 50 | 60 | 70 | 80 | 90 | 100 |

Launching   Evolving   Progressing   Accomplishing   Notable

(Circle Appropriate Percentile)

Zero-Based Organization	**World-Class Organization**
• Organization does not collect data to gauge its customers' concerns with innovative products/ services, and use findings to build better relationships and engagement with various customer groups. • Organization has no concern for gauging customers to improve innovative product/ service offerings and to build better customer engagement and relationships.	• Organization aggregates and trends data regarding customers' perception of the effectiveness of their innovative product/service offerings and services. • Organization collects current levels and trend data of innovative product/service offerings, and uses results to gauge customer loyalty, retention, and positive referrals.

☐ Performance Levels   ☐ Trends   ☐ Comparisons   ☐ Linkage   ☐ Gap

7.2a(2)   The organization's current levels and trends of customer relationship building and engagement as they relate to innovative products/services.

+ Strengths

1.

2.

3.

- Opportunities for Improvement

1.

2.

3.

Corporate Innovation Planning Issues:

Short Term (1 to 2 years)

1.

2.

Long Term (2 years or more)

1.

2.

7.3   Financial and Market Outcomes   (70 pts.)

Summarize your organizations key financial and marketplace performance results by market segments or customer groups, as appropriate, that involve key innovative product/service offerings. Include appropriate comparative data.

QUESTIONS TO ADDRESS

7.3a(1)   What are your organization's current levels and trends of financial performance for key innovative products/services that involve budgetary and financial performance, including aggregate measures of cost containment, financial viability and budgetary performance, as appropriate?

7.3a(2)   What are your organization's current levels and trends of marketplace performance for key innovative products/services, including market share or position, market and market share growth, and new markets entered, as appropriate?

☑ Performance Levels   ☑ Trends   ☑ Comparisons   ☑ Linkage   ☑ Gap

☐ **7.3 Percent Score**

7.3a(1) What are your organization's current levels and trends of financial performance for key innovative products/services that involve budgetary and financial performance, including aggregate measures of cost containment, financial viability and budgetary performance, as appropriate?

Interview notes:

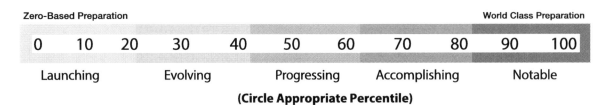

Zero-Based Preparation   World Class Preparation

| 0 | 10 | 20 | 30 | 40 | 50 | 60 | 70 | 80 | 90 | 100 |

Launching   Evolving   Progressing   Accomplishing   Notable

(Circle Appropriate Percentile)

Zero-Based Organization	World-Class Organization
• Organization has not identified a set of key budgetary and financial measures to gauge overall impact of key innovative product/service offerings. Many of the measures are inconsistent and anecdotal. • Organization does not collect trend data on financial performance for key innovative product/service offerings.	• Organization tracks current levels and trends of financial and market performance to gauge overall effectiveness of key innovative product/service offerings. • Organization tracks and trends expenditures per employee, partner, vendor, and customer regarding key innovative product/service offerings. The measures are used to gauge their financial impact against the organization's strategic plans and goals.

☐ Performance Levels   ☐ Trends   ☐ Comparisons   ☐ Linkage   ☐ Gap

7.3a(1) The organization's current levels and trends of financial performance for key innovative products/services, that involve budgetary and financial performance, including aggregate measures of cost containment, financial viability and budgetary performance, as appropriate..

+ Strengths
1.
2.
3.

- Opportunities for Improvement
1.
2.
3.

Corporate Innovation Planning Issues:

Short Term (1 to 2 years)
1.
2.

Long Term (2 years or more)
1.
2.

7.3a(2) What are your organization's current levels and trends of marketplace performance for key innovative products/services, including market share or position, market and market share growth, and new markets entered, as appropriate?

Interview notes:

Zero-Based Preparation   World Class Preparation

0	10	20	30	40	50	60	70	80	90	100

Launching   Evolving   Progressing   Accomplishing   Notable

(Circle Appropriate Percentile)

Zero-Based Organization	World-Class Organization
• Organization has not collected data to gauge its marketplace performance for innovative products/services that have been implemented for its key customers over the past three years. • Organization has not holistically reviewed or collected marketplace performance data on its innovative product/service offerings.	• Organization has a positive three-year trend regarding marketplace performance for its key innovative product/service offerings in existing markets. • Organization has had positive three-year trends in the marketplace for key innovative product/service offerings where new markets were entered.

☐ Performance Levels   ☐ Trends   ☐ Comparisons   ☐ Linkage   ☐ Gap

7.3a(2) The organization's current levels and trends of marketplace performance for key innovative products/services, including market share or position, market and market share growth, and new markets entered, as appropriate.

+ Strengths
1.
2.
3.

- Opportunities for Improvement
1.
2.
3.

Corporate Innovation Planning Issues:
   Short Term (1 to 2 years)
   1.
   2.

   Long Term (2 years or more)
   1.
   2.

7.4 Workforce-Focused Outcomes (70 pts.)

Summarize your organization's key workforce- focused results for workforce engagement and for your workforce environment that is in place regarding corporate innovation initiatives. Segment your results to address the diversity of your workforce and to address your workforce groups and segments, as appropriate. Include appropriate comparative data.

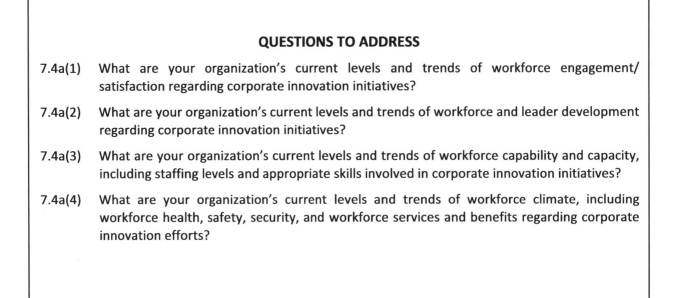

QUESTIONS TO ADDRESS

7.4a(1) What are your organization's current levels and trends of workforce engagement/ satisfaction regarding corporate innovation initiatives?

7.4a(2) What are your organization's current levels and trends of workforce and leader development regarding corporate innovation initiatives?

7.4a(3) What are your organization's current levels and trends of workforce capability and capacity, including staffing levels and appropriate skills involved in corporate innovation initiatives?

7.4a(4) What are your organization's current levels and trends of workforce climate, including workforce health, safety, security, and workforce services and benefits regarding corporate innovation efforts?

7.4 Percent Score

☑Performance Levels ☑Trends ☑Comparisons ☑Linkage ☑Gap

7.4a(1)   What are your organization's current levels and trends of workforce engagement/satisfaction regarding corporate innovation initiatives?

Interview notes:

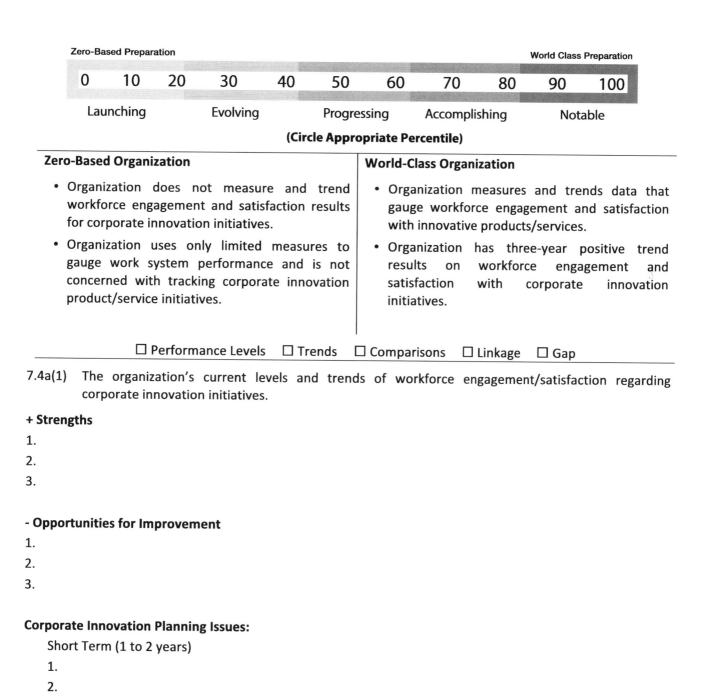

Zero-Based Preparation   World Class Preparation

| 0 | 10 | 20 | 30 | 40 | 50 | 60 | 70 | 80 | 90 | 100 |

Launching   Evolving   Progressing   Accomplishing   Notable

(Circle Appropriate Percentile)

Zero-Based Organization	World-Class Organization
• Organization does not measure and trend workforce engagement and satisfaction results for corporate innovation initiatives. • Organization uses only limited measures to gauge work system performance and is not concerned with tracking corporate innovation product/service initiatives.	• Organization measures and trends data that gauge workforce engagement and satisfaction with innovative products/services. • Organization has three-year positive trend results on workforce engagement and satisfaction with corporate innovation initiatives.

☐ Performance Levels   ☐ Trends   ☐ Comparisons   ☐ Linkage   ☐ Gap

7.4a(1)   The organization's current levels and trends of workforce engagement/satisfaction regarding corporate innovation initiatives.

+ Strengths
1.
2.
3.

- Opportunities for Improvement
1.
2.
3.

Corporate Innovation Planning Issues:
Short Term (1 to 2 years)
1.
2.

Long Term (2 years or more)
1.
2.

7.4a(2)   What are your organization's current levels and trends of workforce and leader development regarding corporate innovation initiatives?

Interview notes:

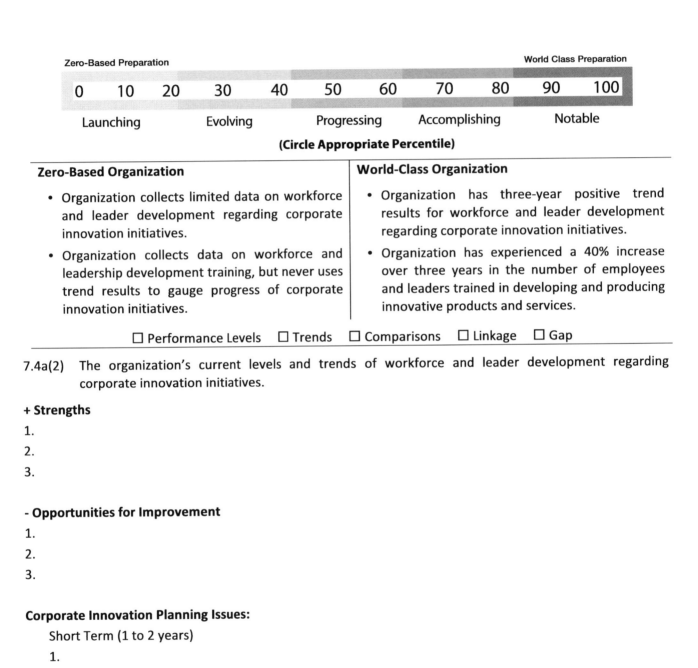

<table>
<tr><td>**Zero-Based Organization**</td><td>**World-Class Organization**</td></tr>
</table>

Zero-Based Organization	World-Class Organization
• Organization collects limited data on workforce and leader development regarding corporate innovation initiatives. • Organization collects data on workforce and leadership development training, but never uses trend results to gauge progress of corporate innovation initiatives.	• Organization has three-year positive trend results for workforce and leader development regarding corporate innovation initiatives. • Organization has experienced a 40% increase over three years in the number of employees and leaders trained in developing and producing innovative products and services.

☐ Performance Levels   ☐ Trends   ☐ Comparisons   ☐ Linkage   ☐ Gap

7.4a(2)   The organization's current levels and trends of workforce and leader development regarding corporate innovation initiatives.

+ Strengths

1.

2.

3.

- Opportunities for Improvement

1.

2.

3.

Corporate Innovation Planning Issues:

   Short Term (1 to 2 years)

   1.

   2.

   Long Term (2 years or more)

   1.

   2.

7.4a(3)   What are your organization's current levels and trends of workforce capability and capacity, including staffing levels and appropriate skills involved in corporate innovation initiatives?

Interview notes:

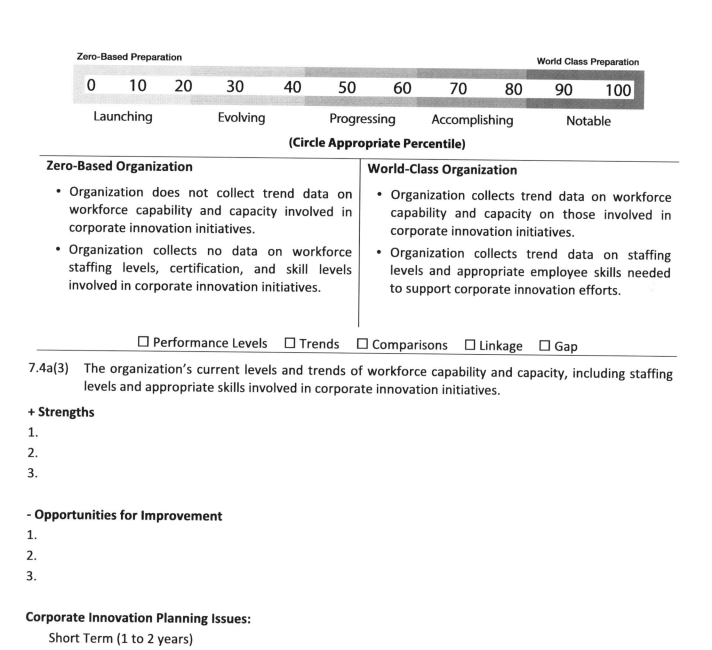

(Circle Appropriate Percentile)

Zero-Based Organization	World-Class Organization
• Organization does not collect trend data on workforce capability and capacity involved in corporate innovation initiatives.	• Organization collects trend data on workforce capability and capacity on those involved in corporate innovation initiatives.
• Organization collects no data on workforce staffing levels, certification, and skill levels involved in corporate innovation initiatives.	• Organization collects trend data on staffing levels and appropriate employee skills needed to support corporate innovation efforts.

☐ Performance Levels   ☐ Trends   ☐ Comparisons   ☐ Linkage   ☐ Gap

7.4a(3)   The organization's current levels and trends of workforce capability and capacity, including staffing levels and appropriate skills involved in corporate innovation initiatives.

+ Strengths
1.
2.
3.

- Opportunities for Improvement
1.
2.
3.

Corporate Innovation Planning Issues:

Short Term (1 to 2 years)
1.
2.

Long Term (2 years or more)
1.
2.

7.4a(4)   What are your organization's current levels and trends of workforce climate, including workforce health, safety, security, and workforce services and benefits regarding corporate innovation efforts?

Interview notes:

Zero-Based Preparation   World Class Preparation

| 0 | 10 | 20 | 30 | 40 | 50 | 60 | 70 | 80 | 90 | 100 |

Launching   Evolving   Progressing   Accomplishing   Notable

(Circle Appropriate Percentile)

Zero-Based Organization	World-Class Organization
• Organization does not gauge workforce well-being, satisfaction, and dissatisfaction regarding corporate innovation efforts. • Organization collects workforce climate data but does not collect data related to workforce health, safety, security, and workforce benefits that are related to corporate innovation efforts.	• Organization collects and trends data on workforce health, safety, security, and workforce services that are related to corporate innovation efforts. • Organization has collected and trended over three years workforce climate results and used findings to improve the overall workforce and their involvement in corporate innovation initiatives.

☐ Performance Levels   ☐ Trends   ☐ Comparisons   ☐ Linkage   ☐ Gap

7.4a(4)   The organization's current levels and trends of workforce climate, including workforce health, safety, security, and workforce services and benefits regarding corporate innovation efforts.

+ Strengths

1.

2.

3.

- Opportunities for Improvement

1.

2.

3.

Corporate Innovation Planning Issues:

Short Term (1 to 2 years)

1.

2.

Longer Term (2 years or more)

1.

2.

7.5   Process Effectiveness Outcomes   (70 pts.)

Summarize your organization's key operational performance results that contribute to the improvement of organizational effectiveness, and corporate innovation, including your organization's readiness for emergencies. Segment your results by customer groups and market segments, and by processes and locations, as appropriate. Include appropriate comparative data.

RESULTS

QUESTIONS TO ADDRESS

7.5a(1)   What are your organization's current levels and trends of operational performance for key work systems and workplace preparedness for disasters or emergencies that impact corporate innovation efforts?

7.5a(2)   What are your organization's current levels and trends in key measures of operational performance of key work processes including productivity, cycle time, and other process measures for effectiveness, and efficiency, that support corporate innovation?

7.5 Percent Score

☑ Performance Levels   ☑ Trends   ☑ Comparisons   ☑ Linkage   ☑ Gap

7.5a(1) What are your organization's current levels and trends of operational performance for key work systems and workplace preparedness for disasters or emergencies that impact corporate innovation efforts?

Interview notes:

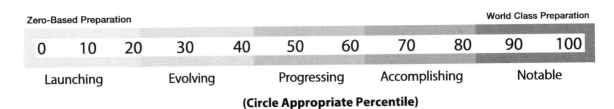

Zero-Based Preparation   World Class Preparation

| 0 | 10 | 20 | 30 | 40 | 50 | 60 | 70 | 80 | 90 | 100 |

Launching   Evolving   Progressing   Accomplishing   Notable

(Circle Appropriate Percentile)

Zero-Based Organization	World-Class Organization
• Organization does not consistently collect key performance results for workplace preparedness. • Organization's measures for key operational results for emergency preparedness is limited and not fully developed data shared or deployed.	• Organization shows positive levels and trends regarding key business continuity measures that support key work systems and workplace preparedness to protect corporate innovation efforts by using a productivity index, known as, Service Quality Indicators (SQIs). • Organization's value creation processes for corporate preparedness for disasters or emergencies that could impact corporate innovation efforts are identified, tracked, and trended to support workplace security and safety.

☐ Performance Levels   ☐ Trends   ☐ Comparisons   ☐ Linkage   ☐ Gap

7.5a(1)   The organization's current levels and trends of operational performance for key work systems and workplace preparedness for disasters or emergencies that impact corporate innovation efforts.

+ Strengths

1.

2.

3.

- Opportunities for Improvement

1.

2.

3.

Corporate Innovation Planning Issues:

Short Term (1 to 2 years)

1.

2.

Long Term (2 years or more)

1.

2.

7.5a(2) What are your organization's current levels and trends in key measures of operational performance of key work processes including productivity, cycle time, and other process measures for effectiveness and efficiency that support corporate innovation?

Interview notes:

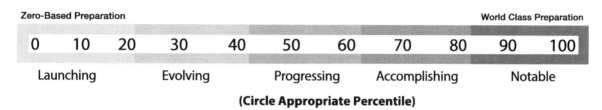

Zero-Based Preparation   **World Class Preparation**

| 0 | 10 | 20 | 30 | 40 | 50 | 60 | 70 | 80 | 90 | 100 |

Launching   Evolving   Progressing   Accomplishing   Notable

(Circle Appropriate Percentile)

Zero-Based Organization	World-Class Organization
• Organization does not collect trend data on operational performance of key support processes. • Organization's trend data collected for operational performance of key support processes has had a negative decrease of 50% over three years.	• Organization's levels and trends of operational performance of key support processes that support corporate innovation have four-year positive trends. • Organization's key measures for operational performance that support corporate innovation goals and objectives have three-year positive trends.

☐ Performance Levels   ☐ Trends   ☐ Comparisons   ☐ Linkage   ☐ Gap

7.5a(2) The organization's current levels and trends in key measures of operational performance of key work processes, including productivity, cycle-time, and other process measures for effectiveness, and efficiency that support corporate innovation.

+ Strengths

1.

2.

3.

- Opportunities for Improvement

1.

2.

3.

Corporate Innovation Planning Issues:

Short Term (1 to 2 years)

1.

2.

Long Term (2 years or more)

1.

2.

7.6   Leadership Outcomes (70 pts.)

Summarize your organization's key governance and senior leadership results that support corporate innovation efforts, including evidence of strategic plan accomplishments, fiscal accountability, legal compliance, ethical behavior, societal responsibility, and corporate intelligence security. Segment your results by organizational units, as appropriate. Include appropriate comparative data.

RESULTS

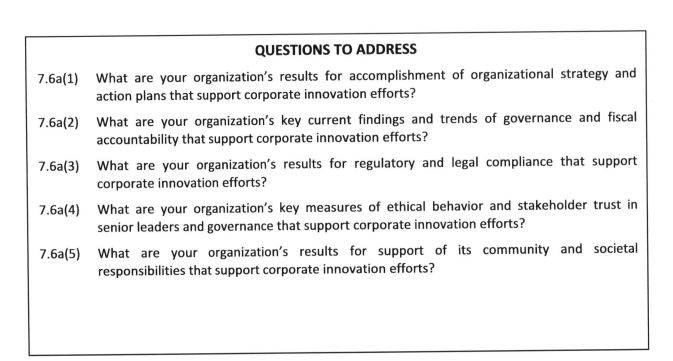

QUESTIONS TO ADDRESS
7.6a(1)   What are your organization's results for accomplishment of organizational strategy and action plans that support corporate innovation efforts?
7.6a(2)   What are your organization's key current findings and trends of governance and fiscal accountability that support corporate innovation efforts?
7.6a(3)   What are your organization's results for regulatory and legal compliance that support corporate innovation efforts?
7.6a(4)   What are your organization's key measures of ethical behavior and stakeholder trust in senior leaders and governance that support corporate innovation efforts?
7.6a(5)   What are your organization's results for support of its community and societal responsibilities that support corporate innovation efforts?

7.6 Percent Score

☑ **Performance Levels**   ☑ **Trends**   ☑ **Comparisons**   ☑ **Linkage**   ☑ **Gap**

7.6a(1)   What are your organization's results for accomplishment of organizational strategy and action plans that support corporate innovation efforts?

Interview notes:

Zero-Based Preparation   World Class Preparation

| 0 | 10 | 20 | 30 | 40 | 50 | 60 | 70 | 80 | 90 | 100 |

Launching   Evolving   Progressing   Accomplishing   Notable

(Circle Appropriate Percentile)

Zero-Based Organization	World-Class Organization
• Organization does not collect results data for accomplishment of its strategies and action plans that support corporate innovation efforts. • Organization has no consistent method for collecting data and measuring results for accomplishment of strategies and action plans that support corporate innovation efforts.	• Organization has accomplished 92% of the strategies and action plans and recognized its staff for completing their strategic objectives that support corporate innovation efforts. • Organization collects results data on completion of strategies and action plans. The organization has experienced a 98% accomplishment rate of action plans that support corporate innovation efforts.

☐ Performance Levels   ☐ Trends   ☐ Comparisons   ☐ Linkage   ☐ Gap

7.6a(1)   The organization's results for accomplishment of organizational strategy and action plans that support corporate innovation efforts.

+ Strengths

1.

2.

3.

- Opportunities for Improvement

1.

2.

3.

Corporate Innovation Planning Issues:

Short Term (1 to 2 years)

1.

2.

Long Term (2 years or more)

1.

2.

7.6a(2) What are your organization's key current findings and trends of governance and fiscal accountability that support corporate innovation efforts?

Interview notes:

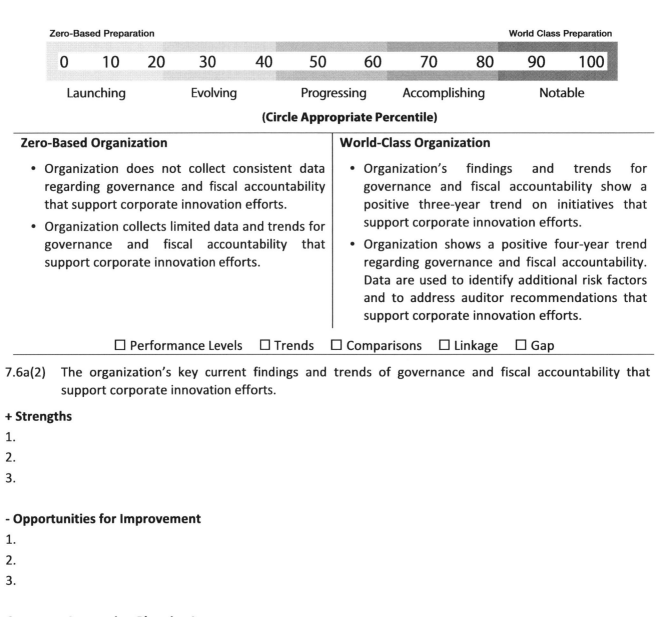

Zero-Based Preparation   **World Class Preparation**

| 0 | 10 | 20 | 30 | 40 | 50 | 60 | 70 | 80 | 90 | 100 |

| Launching | Evolving | Progressing | Accomplishing | Notable |

(Circle Appropriate Percentile)

Zero-Based Organization	World-Class Organization
• Organization does not collect consistent data regarding governance and fiscal accountability that support corporate innovation efforts. • Organization collects limited data and trends for governance and fiscal accountability that support corporate innovation efforts.	• Organization's findings and trends for governance and fiscal accountability show a positive three-year trend on initiatives that support corporate innovation efforts. • Organization shows a positive four-year trend regarding governance and fiscal accountability. Data are used to identify additional risk factors and to address auditor recommendations that support corporate innovation efforts.

☐ Performance Levels   ☐ Trends   ☐ Comparisons   ☐ Linkage   ☐ Gap

7.6a(2)   The organization's key current findings and trends of governance and fiscal accountability that support corporate innovation efforts.

+ Strengths

1.
2.
3.

- Opportunities for Improvement

1.
2.
3.

Corporate Innovation Planning Issues:

Short Term (1 to 2 years)

1.
2.

Long Term (2 years or more)

1.
2.

7.6a(3) What are your organization's results for regulatory and legal compliance that support corporate innovation efforts?

Interview notes:

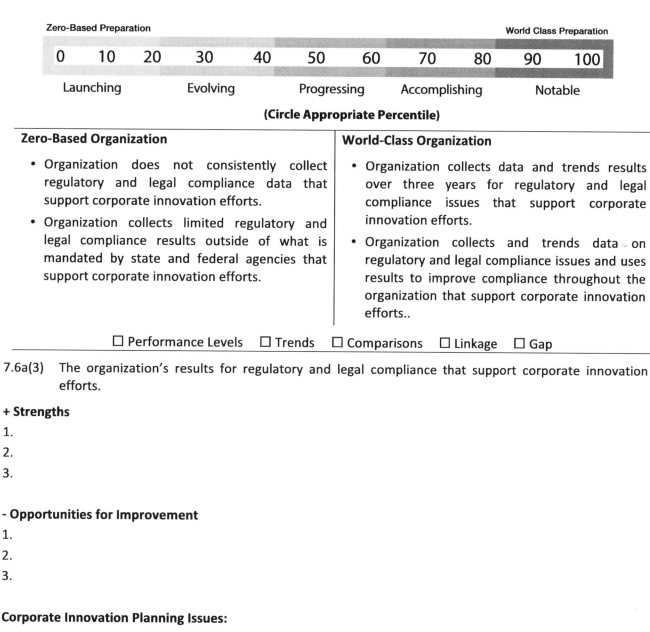

Zero-Based Preparation   World Class Preparation

| 0 | 10 | 20 | 30 | 40 | 50 | 60 | 70 | 80 | 90 | 100 |

Launching   Evolving   Progressing   Accomplishing   Notable

(Circle Appropriate Percentile)

Zero-Based Organization	World-Class Organization
• Organization does not consistently collect regulatory and legal compliance data that support corporate innovation efforts. • Organization collects limited regulatory and legal compliance results outside of what is mandated by state and federal agencies that support corporate innovation efforts.	• Organization collects data and trends results over three years for regulatory and legal compliance issues that support corporate innovation efforts. • Organization collects and trends data on regulatory and legal compliance issues and uses results to improve compliance throughout the organization that support corporate innovation efforts..

☐ Performance Levels   ☐ Trends   ☐ Comparisons   ☐ Linkage   ☐ Gap

7.6a(3)   The organization's results for regulatory and legal compliance that support corporate innovation efforts.

+ Strengths

1.

2.

3.

- Opportunities for Improvement

1.

2.

3.

Corporate Innovation Planning Issues:

Short Term (1 to 2 years)

1.

2.

Long Term (2 years or more)

1.

2.

7.6a(4)   What are your organization's key measures of ethical behavior and stakeholder trust in senior leaders and governance that support corporate innovation efforts?

Interview notes:

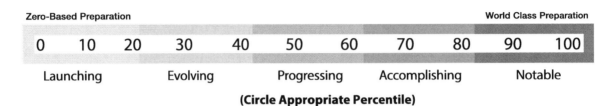

Zero-Based Preparation									World Class Preparation	
0	10	20	30	40	50	60	70	80	90	100
Launching		Evolving			Progressing		Accomplishing		Notable	

(Circle Appropriate Percentile)

Zero-Based Organization	World-Class Organization
• Organization does not have measures in place to gauge ethical behavior and stakeholder trust. Limited policies and procedures are in place that addresses ethical behavior that supports corporate innovation efforts. • Organization collects no data on ethical behavior and stakeholder trust that supports corporate innovation efforts.	• Organization measures senior leaders, employees, customers, partners, and vendors against a documented ethical code of standards that support corporate innovation efforts. • Organization ensures that all senior leaders, employees, partners, vendors, and customers go through a periodic ethics audit regarding adherence to the organization's corporate innovation policies and procedures. Data results are used to gauge overall ethical behavior and stakeholder trust of senior leadership that supports corporate innovation efforts.

☐ Performance Levels   ☐ Trends   ☐ Comparisons   ☐ Linkage   ☐ Gap

7.6a(4)   The organization's key measures of ethical behavior and stakeholder trust in senior leaders and governance that support corporate innovation efforts.

+ Strengths

1.

2.

3.

- Opportunities for Improvement

1.

2.

3.

Corporate Innovation Planning Issues:

Short Term (1 to 2 years)

1.

2.

Long Term (2 years or more)

1.

2.

7.6a(5)   What are your organization's results for support of its community and societal responsibilities that support corporate innovation efforts?

Interview notes:

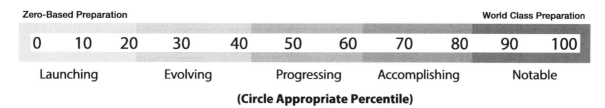

Launching   Evolving   Progressing   Accomplishing   Notable

(Circle Appropriate Percentile)

Zero-Based Organization	World-Class Organization
• Organization does not collect and trend community data to gauge their overall support of community and societal responsibilities that promote corporate innovation efforts.	• Organization collects and trends community and societal initiatives that support corporate innovation efforts and uses the results to gauge on-going progress.
• Organization never considers collecting and trending key indicators that support community involvement and societal responsibilities that support corporate innovation efforts.	• Organization aligns and compares its corporate innovation trends and results with societal and industry results to support an integrated effort in supporting the communities where business is conducted with innovative practices that promote on-going community improvement efforts.

☐ Performance Levels   ☐ Trends   ☐ Comparisons   ☐ Linkage   ☐ Gap

7.6a(5)   The organization's results for support of its community and societal responsibilities that support corporate innovation efforts.

+ Strengths

1.

2.

3.

- Opportunities for Improvement

1.

2.

3.

Corporate Innovation Planning Issues:

Short Term (1 to 2 years)

1.

2.

Long Term (2 years or more)

1.

2.

NOTES

Corporate Innovation Score Sheet
Transfer all assessment item percent scores from the category worksheets.

SUMMARY OF ASSESSMENT ITEMS	Total Points Possible A	Percent Score 0-100% (in 10% units) B	Score (AxB) C
1 Leadership			
1.1 Senior Leadership	70	%	
1.2 Governance and Societal Responsibilities	50	%	
CATEGORY TOTAL	120		
			(Sum C)
2 Strategic Planning			
2.1 Strategy Development	40	%	
2.2 Strategy Deployment	45	%	
CATEGORY TOTAL	85		
			(Sum C)
3 Customer Focus			
3.1 Customer Engagement	40	%	
3.2 Voice of the Customer	45	%	
CATEGORY TOTAL	85		
			(Sum C)
4 Measurement, Analysis, and Knowledge Management			
4.1 Measurement, Analysis, and Improvement of Organizational Performance	45	%	
4.2 Management of Information, Knowledge, and Information Technology	45	%	
CATEGORY TOTAL	90		
			(Sum C)

Continued

SUMMARY OF ASSESSMENT ITEMS	Total Points Possible A	Percent Score 0-100% (in 10% units) B	Score (AxB) C
5 Workforce Focus			
5.1 Workforce Engagement	45	%	
5.2 Workforce Environment	40	%	
CATEGORY TOTAL	85		
			(Sum C)
6 Process Management			
6.1 Work Systems	35	%	
6.2 Work Processes	50	%	
CATEGORY TOTAL	85		
			(Sum C)
7 Results			
7.1 Product/Service Outcomes	100	%	
7.2 Customer Focused Outcomes	70	%	
7.3 Financial and Market Outcomes	70	%	
7.4 Workforce Focused Outcomes	70	%	
7.5 Process Effectiveness Outcomes	70	%	
7.6 Leadership Outcomes	70	%	
CATEGORY TOTAL	450		
			(Sum C)
TOTAL POINTS	1000		

Hierarchy of Corporate Innovation Assessment Needs

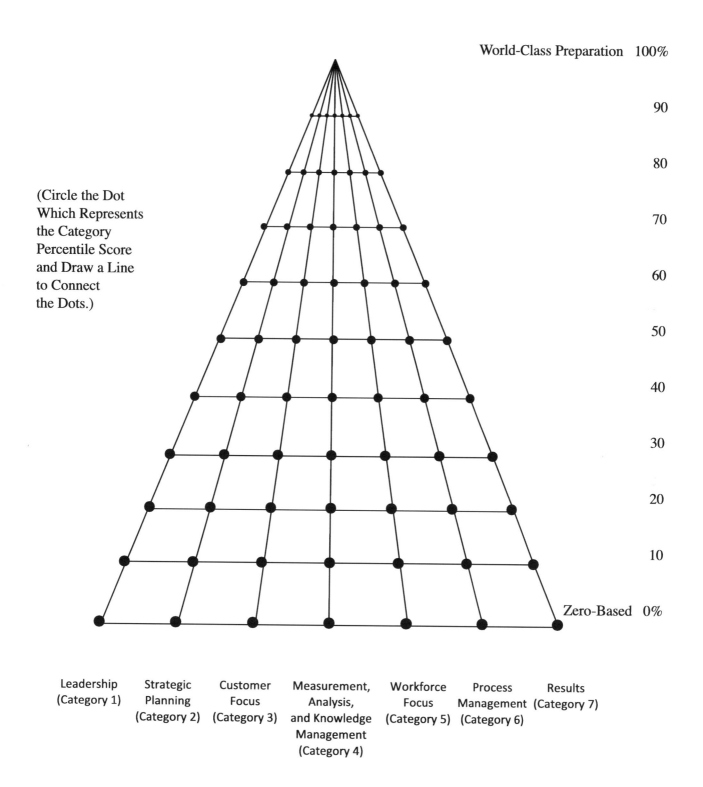

NOTES

10 Transforming Assessment Findings into Actionable Strategies for a Corporate Innovation Plan

The assessment of the organization is complete. The next step is to transform the assessment results into actionable short- and long-term strategies for a corporate innovation plan.

The assessment team should begin this process by reviewing strengths and opportunities for improvement within the areas assessed. The assessment team members will need to reach a consensus on short- and long-term corporate innovation strategic issues for each area. After this process is complete, the team should go back through the assessment manual and collect item percentage scores. The assessment percentages should be shaded within each appropriate item bar graph. Illustrations are given to help the team complete both the assessment bar graphs and strategic planning worksheets.

Organizational Assessment Bar Graph

(Shade in assessment percentages on bar graphs from item score boxes located throughout workbook).

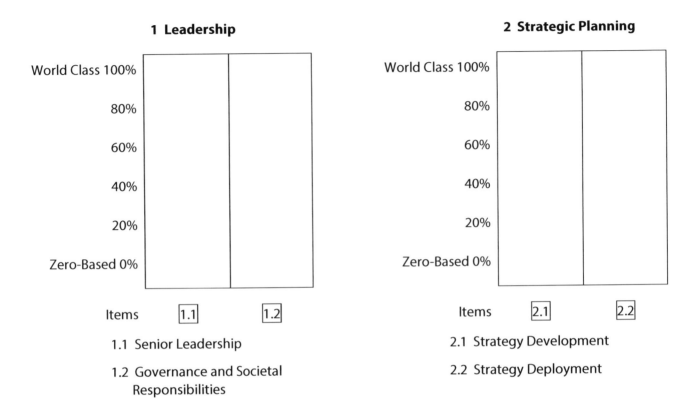

1 Leadership

World Class 100%

80%

60%

40%

20%

Zero-Based 0%

Items   1.1   1.2

1.1 Senior Leadership

1.2 Governance and Societal
     Responsibilities

2 Strategic Planning

World Class 100%

80%

60%

40%

20%

Zero-Based 0%

Items   2.1   2.2

2.1 Strategy Development

2.2 Strategy Deployment

Note: Based on bar graphs, select and prioritize within each category short- and long-term corporate innovation strategic issues identified in the assessment and list below.

1 Leadership
Category

Innovation
Priority 1   _____   Short
                                   Term

                 _____   Long
                                   Term

Innovation
Priority 2   _____   Short
                                   Term

                 _____   Long
                                   Term

Innovation
Priority 3   _____   Short
                                   Term

                 _____   Long
                                   Term

2 Strategic Planning
Category

Innovation
Priority 1   _____   Short
                                   Term

                 _____   Long
                                   Term

Innovation
Priority 2   _____   Short
                                   Term

                 _____   Long
                                   Term

Innovation
Priority 3   _____   Short
                                   Term

                 _____   Long
                                   Term

Organizational Assessment Bar Graph

(Shade in assessment percentages on bar graphs from item score boxes located throughout workbook).

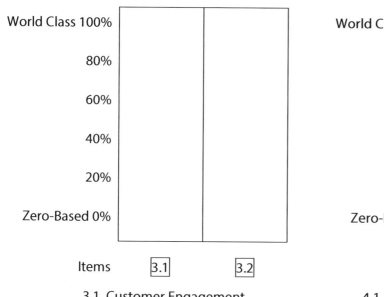

3 Customer Focus

3.1 Customer Engagement

3.2 Voice of the Customer

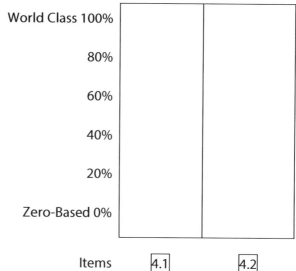

4 Measurement, Analysis, and Knowledge Management

4.1 Measurement , Analysis, and Improvement of Organizational Performance

4.2 Management of Information, Knowledge, and Information Technology

Note: Based on bar graphs, select and prioritize within each category short- and long-term corporate innovation strategic issues identified in the assessment and list below.

3 Customer Focus Category		4 Measurement, Analysis, and Knowledge Management Category	
Innovation Priority 1	Short Term	**Innovation Priority 1**	Short Term
	Long Term		Long Term
Innovation Priority 2	Short Term	**Innovation Priority 2**	Short Term
	Long Term		Long Term
Innovation Priority 3	Short Term	**Innovation Priority 3**	Short Term
	Long Term		Long Term

Organizational Assessment Bar Graph

(Shade in assessment percentages on bar graphs from item score boxes located throughout workbook).

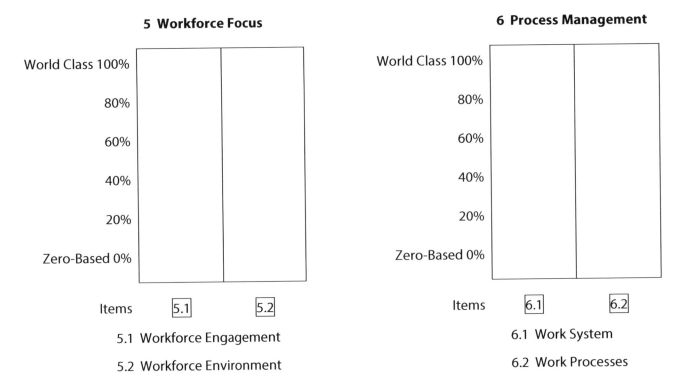

5 Workforce Focus

World Class 100%
80%
60%
40%
20%
Zero-Based 0%

Items 5.1 5.2

5.1 Workforce Engagement

5.2 Workforce Environment

6 Process Management

World Class 100%
80%
60%
40%
20%
Zero-Based 0%

Items 6.1 6.2

6.1 Work System

6.2 Work Processes

Note: Based on bar graphs, select and prioritize within each category short- and long-term corporate innovation strategic issues identified in the assessment and list below.

5 Workforce Focus

Category

Innovation
Priority 1 _____ Short Term
_____ Long Term

Innovation
Priority 2 _____ Short Term
_____ Long Term

Innovation
Priority 3 _____ Short Term
_____ Long Term

6 Process Management

Category

Innovation
Priority 1 _____ Short Term
_____ Long Term

Innovation
Priority 2 _____ Short Term
_____ Long Term

Innovation
Priority 3 _____ Short Term
_____ Long Term

Organizational Assessment Bar Graph

(Shade in assessment percentages on bar graphs from item score boxes located throughout workbook).

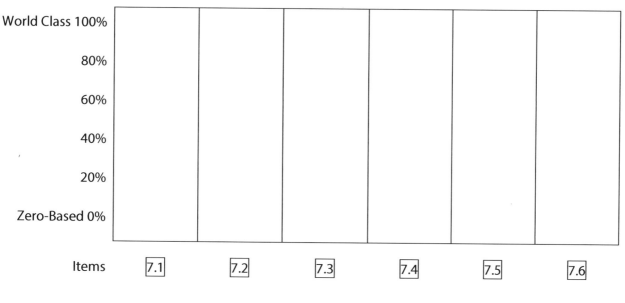

7 Business Results

7.1 Educational Program/Service Outcomes
7.2 Customer-Focused Outcomes
7.3 Financial and Market Outcomes
7.4 Workforce-Focused Outcomes
7.5 Process Effectiveness Outcomes
7.6 Leadership Outcomes

Note: Based on bar graphs, select and prioritize within each category short- and long-term corporate innovation strategic issues identified in the assessment and list below.

7 Results Category

Innovation Priority 1 _____ Short-Term

_____ Long Term

Innovation Priority 2 _____ Short-Term

_____ Long Term

Innovation Priority 3 _____ Short-Term

_____ Long Term

The shaded bar graphs will help the assessment team identify specific items within each category of the organization that need improvement.

After all scores have been shaded in on the bar graphs, the next step for the team is to select and prioritize short- and long-term strategic planning issues within each category that were previously identified through the assessment process by the team. The team will go through the process of prioritizing the strategic short- and long-term planning issues within each category that need to be developed into actionable improvement strategies for the organization (see Illustration #1).

A master strategic planning worksheet for corporate innovation is included in the back of this section. Use this Strategic Planning Worksheet to list your prioritized short- and long-term initiatives. The appropriate category, short or long term, and priority should be circled, detailing the specific initiative. Action item(s) should be listed in respective order to accomplish the identified strategies. In addition, individual responsibilities and review and completion dates should be documented to transform the organization's strategic initiatives into actionable improvement. Illustration #2 details how to complete a strategic planning worksheet for corporate innovation planning.

The strategic planning worksheet for corporate innovation should be completed by the assessment team (see Illustration #2). The results of both the assessment and the identified strategic issues for corporate innovation should be reported back to the organization's senior leadership and ultimately integrated into the organization's annual short- and long-term strategic planning process. See corporate innovation plan and budget forms in Appendix G to develop a complete corporate innovation plan based on assessment findings.

ILLUSTRATION #1

1 Leadership

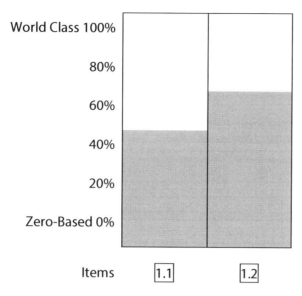

1.1 Senior Leadership

1.2 Governance and
     Societal Responsibilities

Note: Based on bar graphs, select and prioritize within each category short- and long-term strategic issues identified in the assessment and list below.

Innovation

Priority 1	Senior leadership to develop a Corporate Innovation Plan.	Short-Term
	Senior leadership to assess organization for issues and vulnerabilities as they relate to economic vitality of corporate innovation.	Long Term

Innovation Priority 2	Align Corporate Innovation Plan with the organizations strategic planning process.	Short-Term
	President and staff to develop a corporate innovation video that showcases innovative training and leadership development practices.	Long Term

Innovation Priority 3	Revise vision, mission and values statements for corporate innovation.	Short-Term
	Senior management to develop a formal employee recognition system for the organization's corporate innovation plan that promotes community and social responsibility.	Long Term

ILLUSTRATION #2

STRATEGIC PLANNING WORKSHEET FOR A CORPORATE INNOVATION PLAN

Category (circle one)

1 Leadership

2 Strategic Planning

3 Customer Focus

4 Measurement, Analysis and Knowledge
  Management

5 Workforce Focus

6 Process Management

7 Results

Term (circle one)

Short term: one to two years

Long term: more than two years

Priority (circle one) 1 2 3   Senior leadership to develop a Corporate Innovation Plan

ACTION ITEMS (Steps to accomplish strategy)	WHO IS RESPONSIBLE	REVIEW DATE	COMPLETION DATE
1. Identify corporate innovation issues and vulnerabilities.	President	January 10	February 28
2. Form a senior management team to review corporate issues and strategic opportunities.	Vice President	February 5	March 15
3. Cross-functional employee team to word-process and construct the plan.	Director	March 30	April 10
4. Senior staff finalizes Corporate Innovation Plan.	President and Vice Presidents	April 15	May 15
5. Distribute plan to customers, employees, vendors, and partners.	Managers	May 29	June 29
6.			
7.			
8.			
9.			
10.			

List action items in respective order | List individual responsibilities by names or position | List review dates | List completion dates

STRATEGIC PLANNING WORKSHEET FOR A CORPORATE INNOVATION PLAN

Category (circle one)

1 Leadership

2 Strategic Planning

3 Customer Focus

4 Measurement, Analysis, and Knowledge
  Management

5 Workforce Focus

6 Process Management

7 Results

Term (circle one)

Short term: one to two years

Long term: more than two years

Priority (circle one)   1   2   3 _____

ACTION ITEMS (Steps to accomplish strategy)	WHO IS RESPONSIBLE	REVIEW DATE	COMPLETION DATE
1.			
2.			
3.			
4.			
5.			
6.			
7.			
8.			
9.			
10.			

NOTES

NOTES

 **Quick and Easy Vendor/Customer Assessment of Innovative Corporate Practices and Entrepreneurship**

Reasons for Conducting Key Vendor/Customer Assessments

- To coordinate your organization's corporate innovation and entrepreneurial efforts and initiatives with its key vendors/customers to save and reduce costs, improve delivery cycle-time, enhance efficiencies and to ensure a better alignment

- To receive a "results-oriented" organizational review of key vendors/customers and your own organization's innovation and entrepreneurial efforts

- To gain knowledge of the various vendor/customer service quality and innovation and entrepreneurial initiatives that are aligned with your organization

- To identify vendor/customer strengths and opportunities for improvement that can be better aligned with your organization's corporate innovation and entrepreneurial goals and plans

- To improve overall vendor/customer performance and service quality

- To use as a tool to gauge, improve, and manage on-going vendor/customer relationships

- To use assessment results to better align vendors/customers with your organization's corporate innovation and entrepreneurship and short and longer-term strategic plans and goals

- To use as a tool to identify efficiencies, service quality, process improvements and continuous improvement opportunities

- To recognize and reward vendor/customer service excellence and their innovation and entrepreneurial efforts

The Vendor/Customer Assessment ensures that your organization's key vendors and customers strategic plans and goals are aligned with those of your organization's corporate innovation and entrepreneurial goals and directions.

Organizational Profile

Name: _____   Date: _____

Check One:

☐ Vendor   ☐ Customer   ☐ Own Organization

Organizational Environment (Describe the organization's main products, offerings, and services as they relate to innovative corporate practices and entrepreneurship).

Organizational Relationship (Describe how the organization meets the needs of key customer segments, stakeholder groups, vendors, and partners as they relate to innovative corporate practices and entrepreneurship).

Competitive Environment (Describe the organization's competitive position and innovative and entrepreneurial approaches to addressing service quality relative to other comparable organizations delivering similar products, offerings, and services).

Strategic Challenges (Describe the organization's key operations, human resources, community and industry-related challenges that impact innovative corporate practices and entrepreneurship).

Performance Improvement System (Describe the organization's overall approach to performance improvement, and systematic evaluation related to innovative corporate practices and entrepreneurship).

Vendor/Customer Assessment Evaluation Dimensions

The organization scoring system is based on three evaluation dimensions:

(1) approach, (2) deployment, and (3) results. All three dimensions should be considered before assigning a score.

The Three Assessment Dimensions

Approach

Approach refers to the method(s) the organization uses to accomplish its activities and performance initiatives. The scoring criteria used to evaluate the approach may include one or more of the following, as appropriate:

- The effectiveness of the use of methods, tools, and techniques
- The degree to which the approach embodies effective evaluation/improvement cycles
- The degree to which the approach is based upon quantitative information that is objective and reliable
- The degree to which the approach is prevention-based
- The uniqueness and innovativeness of the approach, including significant and effective new adaptations of tools and techniques used in other corporate applications
- The uniqueness of the approach

Deployment

Deployment refers to the extent to which the organization applies and/or distributes its activities and performance initiatives among employees, customers, vendors, stakeholders, and/or departments. The scoring criteria used to evaluate deployment may include one or more of the following, as appropriate:

- The appropriate and effective application among employees, customers, suppliers, stakeholders, and/or departments
- The appropriate and effective application to all transactions and interactions with employees, customers, suppliers, stakeholders, and/or departments
- The activity involves all employees
- The activity is applied in all departments

Results

Results refers to outcomes the organization achieves when applying their activities and performance initiatives. The scoring criteria used to evaluate results may include one or more of the following, as appropriate:

- The rate of quality and performance improvement
- The breadth of quality and performance improvement
- The demonstration of sustained performance improvement
- The comparison with competitive and/or "Best Practice" organization initiatives
- The organization's ability to show that improvement results were derived from its strategic initiatives.

Guidelines for the vendor/Customer Assessment

Introduction

The assessment is a carefully considered evaluation resulting in an opinion or judgment of the effectiveness and efficiency of the organization and the maturity of the organization's performance management system. Self-Assessment is usually performed by the organization's own employees. The intent of the assessment is to provide fact-based guidance to the organization regarding where to invest resources for innovative and entrepreneurial products/services and/or activities and improvement in overall service quality.

The assessment is intended to provide an approach to determine the relative degree of maturity of the organization's quality system and to identify the main areas of improvement. Specific features of the organizational self-assessment approach are that it can:

- be applied to gauge the organization's overall innovative and entrepreneurial initiatives,

- be completed quickly with internal resources,

- be completed by a multi-disciplinary team, or by one person in the organization who is supported by senior leadership,

- identify and facilitate the prioritization of the organization's strengths and opportunities for improvement and identification of corporate innovation and entrepreneurial planning issues, and

- facilitate maturing and aligning of the organization's corporate innovation and entrepreneurial activities and ultimately improving overall performance excellence.

Vendor/Customer Self-Assessment Scoring Profile

Approach/Deployment

Maturity Level	Performance Level	Guidance
0	Approach	No Approach/Anecdotal
1 (Launching)	Approach	Good Approach/No Deployment
2 (Evolving)	Approach	Systematic Approach/ Not Fully Deployed
3 (Progressing)	Deployment	Sound Approach/ Partial Deployment
4 (Accomplishing)	Deployment	Sound Approach/ Mostly Deployed
5 (Notable)	Deployment	Sound Approach/ Full Deployment

Results

Maturity Level	Performance Level	Guidance
0	Results	No Performance Results/ Anecdotal
1 (Launching)	Results	Some Performance Results
2 (Evolving)	Results	Good Performance Results
3 (Progressing)	Results	Some Trends/ Good Results
4 (Accomplishing)	Results	Many Improvement Trends/ Good Results
5 (Notable)	Results	Excellent Trends/ Sustained Results

Assessment Innovation Plan

List strengths and opportunities based on assessment. Align and transform key findings into a corporate innovation plan.

Strengths

Opportunities

Corporate innovation and entrepreneurial Planning Issues

  Short Term (1 to 2 years)

  1.

  2.

  Long Term (2 years or more)

  1.

  2.

1 Leadership
(Circle one)

✓ Documentation

1. Senior Leadership sets and deploys the organization's innovation and entrepreneurial values, strategic directions, and performance expectations to all key stakeholders.

0	1	2	3	4	5
Approach			Deployment		

2. Senior Leaders create an environment for empowerment, innovation, entrepreneurship and equity for all employees.

0	1	2	3	4	5
Approach			Deployment		

3. Organization's corporate ethics and accountability issues are addressed by senior leadership (i.e. management accountability for the organization's actions, fiscal accountability, independent internal/external audits, and protection of stakeholder interests.)

0	1	2	3	4	5
Approach			Deployment		

4. Senior leaders review the organization's corporate performance and capabilities, innovative practices and entrepreneurship relative to competitors and comparable organizations short/longer term goals, and achievements.

0	1	2	3	4	5
Approach			Deployment		

5. Senior leaders identify, review, and share with stakeholders key performance measures on a regular basis that include measures/indicators of achievement of the organizations strategy and action plans.

0	1	2	3	4	5
Approach			Deployment		

6. Senior leaders translate key performance review findings into priorities for legal, regulatory, and accreditation results.

0	1	2	3	4	5
Approach			Deployment		

7. Organization's leadership is reviewed by key stakeholders and the findings are used to improve their leadership effectiveness.

0	1	2	3	4	5
Approach			Deployment		

8. The organization anticipates and addresses the impact that its corporate programs, offerings, services and operations have on the communities it serves both currently and in the future.

0	1	2	3	4	5
Approach			Deployment		

9. The organization ensures ethical behavior in all transactions and interactions involving employees, customers and vendor initiatives.

0	1	2	3	4	5
Approach			Deployment		

10. The organization actively supports innovation and entrepreneurship within its industry.

0	1	2	3	4	5
Approach			Deployment		

To score, add the circled numbers together and divide by 10.
Transfer score to (Supplement 1) Radar Graph.

Average Score

Note: List documents that support assessment findings.

Assessment Innovation Plan

List strengths and opportunities based on assessment. Align and transform key findings into a corporate innovation plan.

Strengths

Opportunities

Corporate Innovation and entrepreneurial Planning Issues

Short Term (1 to 2 years)

1.

2.

Long Term (2 years or more)

1.

2.

2 Strategic Planning
(Circle one)

✓ Documentation

1. The organization's overall strategic planning process for innovation and entrepreneurial practices involves all key stakeholders.

0	1	2	3	4	5
Approach			Deployment		

2. The organization's strategic planning process addresses environmental issues, program offerings, technology, resources, budgetary, ethical responsibilities, vendor/customer needs, innovation, and entrepreneurship issues.

0	1	2	3	4	5
Approach			Deployment		

3. The organization has documented its strategic objectives in their corporate plan and has published a timetable for accomplishing them.

0	1	2	3	4	5
Approach			Deployment		

4. The organization's strategic objectives listed in their corporate plan balance the needs of employees and key stakeholders.

0	1	2	3	4	5
Approach			Deployment		

5. The organization has developed and deployed action plans to employees to achieve key innovative and entrepreneurial objectives .

0	1	2	3	4	5
Approach			Deployment		

6. The organization has identified and shared with all key stakeholders its short and longer-term action plans.

0	1	2	3	4	5
Approach			Deployment		

7. The organization has identified human resource plans within its strategic objectives and has published action plans to ensure progress toward meeting its goals. Employees are recognized for completing their goals.

0	1	2	3	4	5
Approach			Deployment		

8. The organization has identified key performance indicators for tracking action plan progress of its strategic plan accomplishments.

0	1	2	3	4	5
Approach			Deployment		

9. The organization has identified performance projections with time horizons for its strategic objectives.

0	1	2	3	4	5
Approach			Deployment		

10. The organization has based its short and longer-term performance projections for innovative corporate practices and entrepreneurship on competitors, comparable organizations, benchmarks, goals, and/or past performance.

0	1	2	3	4	5
Approach			Deployment		

To score, add the circled numbers together and divide by 10.
Transfer score to (Supplement 1) Radar Graph.

Average Score

Note: List documents that support assessment findings.

Assessment Innovation Plan

List strengths and opportunities based on assessment. Align and transform key findings into a corporate innovation plan.

Strengths

Opportunities

Corporate Innovation and Entrepreneurial Planning Issues

Short Term (1 to 2 years)

1.

2.

Long Term (2 years or more)

1.

2.

3 Customer Focus
(Circle one)

✓ Documentation

1. The organization has a method to determine and target customer segments and markets for innovative corporate practices and entrepreneurship.

0	1	2	3	4	5
Approach			Deployment		

2. The organization has methods in place to listen and learn from current, former, and future customers and stakeholders regarding innovative and entrepreneurial requirements and expectations.

0	1	2	3	4	5
Approach			Deployment		

3. The organization keeps its listening and learning methods current with customer needs and directions (i.e., focus groups, surveys, benchmark visits, etc.)

0	1	2	3	4	5
Approach			Deployment		

4. The organization collects and trends data on customer relationships regarding innovative and entrepreneurial offerings.

0	1	2	3	4	5
Approach			Deployment		

5. The organization ensures that a consistent customer relationship management approach is in place for employees who have direct contact with customers/stakeholders.

0	1	2	3	4	5
Approach			Deployment		

6. The organization ensures that its customer relationship skills are kept current with consistent changing of service needs and directions.

0	1	2	3	4	5
Approach			Deployment		

7. The organization has a consistent method in place to determine customer satisfaction and dissatisfaction with innovative and entrepreneurial programs and services provided.

0	1	2	3	4	5
Approach			Deployment		

8. The organization has a consistent customer follow-up procedure for its programs, services, and offerings that ensures prompt and actionable feedback.

0	1	2	3	4	5
Approach			Deployment		

9. The organization compares customer satisfaction with product/service delivery against competitive and/or comparable organizations that deliver similar services.

0	1	2	3	4	5
Approach			Deployment		

10. The organization keeps its methods for determining customer satisfaction with products/services current with service needs and directions (i.e., focus groups, surveys, etc.).

0	1	2	3	4	5
Approach			Deployment		

To score, add the circled numbers together and divide by 10. Transfer score to (Supplement 1) Radar Graph.

Average Score

Note: List documents that support assessment findings.

Assessment Innovation Plan

List strengths and opportunities based on assessment. Align and transform key findings into a corporate innovation plan.

Strengths

Opportunities

Corporate Innovation and Entrepreneurial Planning Issues

    Short Term (1 to 2 years)

    1.

    2.

    Long Term (2 years or more)

    1.

    2.

4 Measurement, Analysis, and Knowledge Management

(Circle one)

✓ **Documentation**

1. The organization selects, collects, aligns, and integrates corporate data and information for tracking daily operations of innovative and entrepreneurial offerings.

0	1	2	3	4	5
Approach			Deployment		

2. The organization has a selection process to collect key comparative data and information to support and protect operational, strategic decision making, and innovation and entrepreneurship.

0	1	2	3	4	5
Approach			Deployment		

3. The organization keeps its performance measurement system current with organization needs and directions.

0	1	2	3	4	5
Approach			Deployment		

4. The organization collects data and information that support senior leadership's direction to accomplish the organization's strategic plans and directions.

0	1	2	3	4	5
Approach			Deployment		

5. The organization's leadership communicates to employees corporate data and information results that support its decision making and strategic decisions for innovative and entrepreneurial offerings.

0	1	2	3	4	5
Approach			Deployment		

6. The organization makes needed corporate data and information accessible for employees, stakeholders, and customers.

0	1	2	3	4	5
Approach			Deployment		

7. The organization ensures that hardware and software are reliable, secure, user-friendly.

0	1	2	3	4	5
Approach			Deployment		

8. The organization keeps data and information mechanisms, including hardware and software systems, current with its corporate needs and directions.

0	1	2	3	4	5
Approach			Deployment		

9. The organization manages the collection and transfer of innovative and entrepreneurial knowledge among employees, stakeholders, and vendors/customers.

0	1	2	3	4	5
Approach			Deployment		

10. The organization ensures that its data, information, organizational knowledge, and intellectual capital related to innovation and entrepreneurship is protected, timely, reliable, secure, accurate, confidential, and has integrity.

0	1	2	3	4	5
Approach			Deployment		

To score, add the circled numbers together and divide by 10.
Transfer score to (Supplement 1) Radar Graph.

Average Score

Note: List documents that support assessment findings.

Assessment Innovation Plan

List strengths and opportunities based on assessment. Align and transform key findings into a corporate innovation plan.

Strengths

Opportunities

Corporate Innovation and Entrepreneurial Planning Issues

   Short Term (1 to 2 years)

   1.

   2.

   Long Term (2 years or more)

   1.

   2.

5 Workforce Focus
(Circle one)

✓ **Documentation**

1. The organization organizes, manages, and communicates initiatives that promote cooperation, initiative, empowerment, and innovation and entrepreneurship among employees.

0	1	2	3	4	5
Approach			Deployment		

2. The organization's performance management system supports and recognizes high-performance work among employees and employee teams regarding innovative corporate practices and entrepreneurship.

0	1	2	3	4	5
Approach			Deployment		

3. The organization identifies characteristics and skills in its recruiting, hiring, retaining, and career progression of employees.

0	1	2	3	4	5
Approach			Deployment		

4. The organization's employee education and training contribute to achievement of action plans and directions that promote a well-trained and highly skilled workforce.

0	1	2	3	4	5
Approach			Deployment		

5. The organization ensures that innovation and Entrepreneurship education/training is given to its employees.

0	1	2	3	4	5
Approach			Deployment		

6. The organization rewards employees who promote high performance and innovative corporate practices and entrepreneurship.

0	1	2	3	4	5
Approach			Deployment		

7. The organization reviews and improves innovative and corporate practices related to workplace health, safety and security issues.

0	1	2	3	4	5
Approach			Deployment		

8. The organization addresses corporate issues/concerns during times of a crisis and/or emergency in their Business Continuity planning.

0	1	2	3	4	5
Approach			Deployment		

9. The organization has an assessment process to determine employee well-being, satisfaction, and motivation regarding innovative corporate practices and entrepreneurship.

0	1	2	3	4	5
Approach			Deployment		

10. The organization uses assessment findings to identify and gauge workforce development issues and innovative and entrepreneurial opportunities that need to be addressed.

0	1	2	3	4	5
Approach			Deployment		

☐ _____
☐ _____
☐ _____
☐ _____
☐ _____
☐ _____
☐ _____
☐ _____
☐ _____
☐ _____
☐ _____
☐ _____
☐ _____
☐ _____
☐ _____

Note: List documents that support assessment findings.

To score, add the circled numbers together and divide by 10. Transfer score to (Supplement 1) Radar Graph.

Average Score

Assessment Innovation Plan

List strengths and opportunities based on assessment. Align and transform key findings into a corporate innovation plan.

Strengths

Opportunities

Corporate Innovation and Entrepreneurial Planning Issues

Short Term (1 to 2 years)

1.

2.

Long Term (2 years or more)

1.

2.

6 Process Management
(Circle one)

✓ **Documentation**

1. The organization determines innovative and entrepreneurial processes that address market needs and directions for employees and stakeholders (i.e., technology skills, problem-solving skills, team involvement, etc.)

0	1	2	3	4	5
Approach			Deployment		

2. The organization determines corporate innovation and entrepreneurial process requirements by incorporating input from employees, vendors, stakeholders, and partners.

0	1	2	3	4	5
Approach			Deployment		

3. The organization incorporates new technology and organizational knowledge into a formal design methodology for all innovative and entrepreneurial projects.

0	1	2	3	4	5
Approach			Deployment		

4. The organization has key performance measures in place to control and improve its innovative and entrepreneurial processes.

0	1	2	3	4	5
Approach			Deployment		

5. The organization reviews its innovative and entrepreneurial processes to maximize success and improve its programs, offerings, and services.

0	1	2	3	4	5
Approach			Deployment		

6. The organization determines key support processes for each core process (i.e., facilities management, secretarial, food service, etc.)

0	1	2	3	4	5
Approach			Deployment		

7. The organization determines key support process requirements for innovative and entrepreneurial products/services by incorporating input from employees, stakeholders, and partners.

0	1	2	3	4	5
Approach			Deployment		

8. The organization incorporates new technology and organizational knowledge into the design of both support and core processes to ensure state-of-the-art practices are in place.

0	1	2	3	4	5
Approach			Deployment		

9. The organization has in place performance measures to control and improve support processes of key innovative and entrepreneurial products/services.

0	1	2	3	4	5
Approach			Deployment		

10. The organization reviews its support processes to achieve better performance, to reduce variability, and to keep them current with its corporate needs and directions.

0	1	2	3	4	5
Approach			Deployment		

To score, add the circled numbers together and divide by 10. Transfer score to (Supplement 1) Radar Graph.

Average Score

Note: List documents that support assessment findings.

Assessment Innovation Plan

List strengths and opportunities based on assessment. Align and transform key findings into a corporate innovation plan.

Strengths

Opportunities

Corporate Innovation and Entrepreneurial Planning Issues

 Short Term (1 to 2 years)

  1.

  2.

 Long Term (2 years or more)

  1.

  2.

7 Results
(Circle one)

✓ **Documentation**

1. The organization collects and trends key supply chain management results data on all innovative and entrepreneurial products/services.

0	1	2	3	4	5
Results

2. The organization collects and trends vendor/customer and stakeholder satisfaction/dissatisfaction data on all innovative and entrepreneurial products/ services and compares the data against competitive or comparable organizations.

0	1	2	3	4	5
Results

3. The organization collects and trends budgetary, financial performance, and market performance results data (i.e. liquidity, days cash on hand, asset utilization

0	1	2	3	4	5
Results

4. The organization collects and trends customer service data on its innovative and entrepreneurial products/services..

0	1	2	3	4	5
Results

5. The organization collects and trends performance and effectiveness results data (i.e, knowledge, and skill-sharing results, etc.)

0	1	2	3	4	5
Results

6. The organization collects and trends employee well-being, satisfaction, and dissatisfaction, workforce capability/ capacity, workforce climate/engagement, and emergency preparedness data.

0	1	2	3	4	5
Results

7. The organization collects and trends process effectiveness and efficiency data on innovative and entrepreneurial products/services..

0	1	2	3	4	5
Results

8. The organization collects and trends operational performance of key support service results (i.e., productivity, cycle time, vendor/customer performance, etc.)

0	1	2	3	4	5
Results

9. The organization collects and trends results data for fiscal accountability, ethical behavior, and legal compliance and all innovative and entrepreneurial products/services.

0	1	2	3	4	5
Results

10. The organization collects and trends results data for its community and industry involvement in promoting innovation and entrepreneurship.

0	1	2	3	4	5
Results

To score, add the circled numbers together and divide by 10.
Transfer score to (Supplement 1) Radar Graph.

Average Score

Note: List documents that support assessment findings.

Supplement 1 – Radar Graph

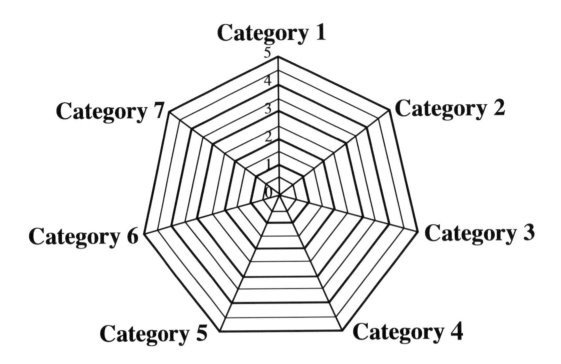

Category 1 **Leadership**

Category 2 **Strategic Planning**

Category 3 **Customer Focus**

Category 4 **Measurement, Analysis, and Knowledge Management**

Category 5 **Workforce Focus**

Category 6 **Process Management**

Category 7 **Results**

Note: Record average scores from the assessment onto the above radar graph.

Scoring Profile

Zero-Based Preparation   **World Class Preparation**

| 0 | 10 | 20 | 30 | 40 | 50 | 60 | 70 | 80 | 90 | 100 |

Launching   Evolving   Progressing   Accomplishing   Notable

(**Average all category scores, divide by 7, and circle appropriate number. Refer to Corporate Innovation Scoring Profiles section in Chapter 1 for score descriptions**).

Organization: _____

Employees Involved: _____

Date: _____

B Corporate Innovation Benchmarking Process

Corporate Innovation Benchmarking Process

Place a check next to each step completed.

Benchmarking Team Formation

_____ 1. Form a corporate innovation benchmarking team.

_____ 2. Identify corporate processes that need to improve.

_____ 3. List in priority order corporate processes that offer the greatest opportunity for improvement through innovation.

_____ 4. Select Corporate processes from the prioritized list.

_____ 5. Develop a list of organizations that are known for best practices regarding the identified processes.

_____ 6. Reach a consensus on a maximum of three organizations to consider for a benchmark visit (Form 2).

_____ 7. Mail out, e-mail, or fax benchmarking surveys to organizations identified by the team as exhibiting best practices (use "Benchmarking survey", Form 1).

_____ 8. Team collects benchmarking survey data (collect data on Form 1).

_____ 9. Team reaches a consensus on survey scores.

_____ 10. Record survey scores on graphs (top half of Form 2).

_____ 11. Select benchmarking visits based on graph comparisons (minimum of three).

Benchmarking Site Visit

_____ 12.Team leader sends a formal letter requesting a site visit (Note: Request no more than a three-hour visit).

_____ 13.Send site visit questions with the letter requesting a site visit (base questions on benchmarking survey).

_____ 14.Request in advance any information that the host organization would like to secure from the visiting organization (all approvals must be secured from senior leadership before the site visit is made).

_____ 15.Select two or three team members for each site visit.

_____ 16.After all site visits have been approved, secure travel and accommodations for team members at each site.

_____ 17.Collect and place all pamphlets, handouts, and data received from site visit into a benchmarking folder. All findings are to be shared back onsite with the entire team.

_____ 18.Team leader sends a "thank you" letter to the host organization that was benchmarked.

Benchmarking Site Visit Completed

_____ 19.Review all data collected from each site visit.

_____ 20.List key findings from each site visit ("Site Visit Benchmarking Overview", Form 3).

_____ 21.Review and reach a consensus on site visit findings.

_____ 22.Incorporate findings into process improvement ("Benchmark and Process Improvement Steps", Form 4).

Form 1: Benchmarking Survey

Name of Organization: _____   Date of Phone Call/E-mail: _____

Name/ Title of Person Interviewed:_____

This telephone or e-mail survey includes a series of questions to help the benchmark team determine which identified best practice site to visit. The highest possible score achievable by an organization is 50 points. Write the comments in the space provided; then rate the answer.

Rating   Scale

Do Not | | | | World
Know | | | | Class

1	2	3	4	5	Best Practice to be Benchmarked_____
1	2	3	4	5	Do you consider your processes the "best practice" within your industry? Why or why not?_____
1	2	3	4	5	Would you rate your processes against competitors' organizations as being excellent, good, or fair? _____ Why? _____
1	2	3	4	5	How does your organization determine that your processes are "best practice" within your industry?_____
1	2	3	4	5	Does your organization collect process results? _____ Will you share your results? _____
1	2	3	4	5	Have other organizations benchmarked your corporate processes? _____
1	2	3	4	5	How often are your corporate processes reviewed and benchmarked against other identified best practices inside or outside your organization? _____
1	2	3	4	5	Does your organization maintain a budget for your processes?
1	2	3	4	5	How many employees are involved in maintaining your corporate processes? _____
1	2	3	4	5	How do your corporate processes contribute to increasing overall competitiveness for your organization? _____
1	2	3	4	5	What impact do your processes have on your overall organizational effectiveness? ___

☐ Total Points

Form 2: Benchmarking Survey Results Graph

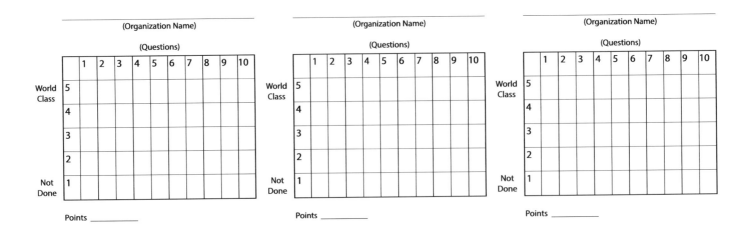

Note: Place a dot under each survey question number that best reflects the score from the survey (Form 1). Draw a line to connect the dots.

SITE VISIT SELECTIONS
(Based on benchmarking survey results)

Organization _____   Team Leader _____

Location _____   Team Members _____

Date _____   _____

Organization _____   Team Leader _____

Location _____   Team Members _____

Date _____   _____

Organization _____   Team Leader _____

Location _____   Team Members _____

Date _____   _____

Form 3: Site Visit Benchmarking Overview

Process Benchmarked _____

Organization Location _____

Date _____

Key Findings _____

_____

_____

_____

Process Benchmarked _____

Organization Location _____

Date _____

Key Findings _____

_____

_____

_____

Process Benchmarked _____

Organization Location _____

Date _____

Key Findings _____

_____

_____

_____

Form 4: Benchmarked Process Improvement Steps

Process Benchmarked: _____

Organization Benchmarked: _____

Proposed steps to be incorporated into an improved process based on site visits. Use one form for each process identified for improvement.

	Process Steps (Present)	Process Steps (Based on site visits)	Process Steps (Improved)
1			
2			
3			
4			
5			
6			
7			
8			
9			
10			

C Checklist for 100 Corporate Innovation Considerations to Benchmark

_____ 1. Review corporate innovative best practices and processes off selected corporations.

_____ 2. Identify and select supply chain management innovative processes/practices of various corporations.

_____ 3. Review and analyze to what extent select corporations protect their intellectual capital and trademarked/copyrighted innovative products and service offerings.

_____ 4. Review various methods organizations use to measure innovation performance.

_____ 5. Review how organizations protect their innovative practices through patent submission.

_____ 6. Review noted corporate strategic planning processes of organizations that promote corporate innovation.

_____ 7. Review how revenue growth is projected for innovative products/services.

_____ 8. Investigate how organizations collect their idea submissions and flow regarding innovative practices.

_____ 9. Review select organization's time-to-market timeline for innovative products/services that have been produced.

_____ 10. Review select organization's conversion rate of patents into products and how they measure success of their innovations.

_____ 11. Investigate the application of an innovation index.

_____ 12. Investigate the multiple factors that select organizations contribute to innovation.

_____ 13. Benchmark organizations' innovation results.

_____ 14. Review corporate budgets that are devoted to innovation initiatives.

_____ 15. Review various organizations' innovation framework.

_____ 16. Review strategies used by notable organizations in launching an innovative culture.

_____ 17. Review various corporate business models of organizations known to promote innovative practices.

_____ 18. Review various business cases that address corporate innovation.

_____ 19. Review innovation funding for select organizations.

_____ 20. Investigate the use of the Index of Corporate Innovation (ICI) as a diagnostic tool to measure an organization's innovation capabilities and performance.

_____ 21. Investigate how various corporate innovation processes are selected and funded.

_____ 22. Review various corporate leadership structures of noted organizations known for their innovative practices.

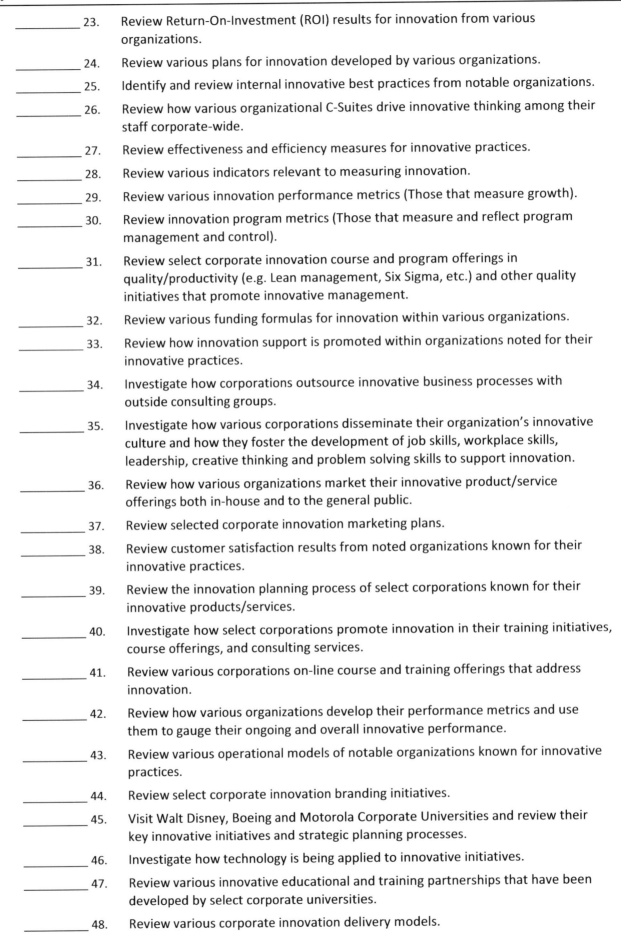

_____ 23. Review Return-On-Investment (ROI) results for innovation from various organizations.

_____ 24. Review various plans for innovation developed by various organizations.

_____ 25. Identify and review internal innovative best practices from notable organizations.

_____ 26. Review how various organizational C-Suites drive innovative thinking among their staff corporate-wide.

_____ 27. Review effectiveness and efficiency measures for innovative practices.

_____ 28. Review various indicators relevant to measuring innovation.

_____ 29. Review various innovation performance metrics (Those that measure growth).

_____ 30. Review innovation program metrics (Those that measure and reflect program management and control).

_____ 31. Review select corporate innovation course and program offerings in quality/productivity (e.g. Lean management, Six Sigma, etc.) and other quality initiatives that promote innovative management.

_____ 32. Review various funding formulas for innovation within various organizations.

_____ 33. Review how innovation support is promoted within organizations noted for their innovative practices.

_____ 34. Investigate how corporations outsource innovative business processes with outside consulting groups.

_____ 35. Investigate how various corporations disseminate their organization's innovative culture and how they foster the development of job skills, workplace skills, leadership, creative thinking and problem solving skills to support innovation.

_____ 36. Review how various organizations market their innovative product/service offerings both in-house and to the general public.

_____ 37. Review selected corporate innovation marketing plans.

_____ 38. Review customer satisfaction results from noted organizations known for their innovative practices.

_____ 39. Review the innovation planning process of select corporations known for their innovative products/services.

_____ 40. Investigate how select corporations promote innovation in their training initiatives, course offerings, and consulting services.

_____ 41. Review various corporations on-line course and training offerings that address innovation.

_____ 42. Review how various organizations develop their performance metrics and use them to gauge their ongoing and overall innovative performance.

_____ 43. Review various operational models of notable organizations known for innovative practices.

_____ 44. Review select corporate innovation branding initiatives.

_____ 45. Visit Walt Disney, Boeing and Motorola Corporate Universities and review their key innovative initiatives and strategic planning processes.

_____ 46. Investigate how technology is being applied to innovative initiatives.

_____ 47. Review various innovative educational and training partnerships that have been developed by select corporate universities.

_____ 48. Review various corporate innovation delivery models.

_____ 49.   Review various stages of development and progression of corporate innovation within organizations noted for their innovative practices.

_____ 50.   Investigate how firms enhance their innovative performance.

_____ 51.   Review training and development curriculum that addresses corporate innovation.

_____ 52.   Review various innovation strategies of successful organizations.

_____ 53.   Review business investment in innovation strategies.

_____ 54.   Investigate the benefits of protecting intellectual property and the investment in innovation.

_____ 55.   Review various corporate award programs that recognize innovation within the workforce.

_____ 56.   Review corporate training and employee development programs that are responsible for developing people and growing the organization's capacity to increase innovative thinkers who incorporate the use of problem-solving skills and metrics to develop and deliver innovative products/services.

_____ 57.   Review various corporate employee handbooks that address innovative practices among the workforce.

_____ 58.   Review select corporate Policies and Procedures Manuals that address innovation.

_____ 59.   Review select organizations planning process in creating in-house innovation teams.

_____ 60.   Review select corporate curriculum development and program design methodologies that address innovation.

_____ 61.   Visit organizations that have commercialized their innovative business opportunities.

_____ 62.   Review various corporate policies and procedures that address innovation.

_____ 63.   Review national/regional innovation systems that support the generation and diffusion of innovation to raise its role in economic development.

_____ 64.   Review joint efforts by public and private sector (public/private partnerships) that are efficient and effective in developing innovative initiatives.

_____ 65.   Review the long-term financial impact on select corporate innovation initiatives.

_____ 66.   Investigate staffing issues for innovation of organizations known for their innovative practices.

_____ 67.   Investigate the percent of employees assigned to innovation activities/efforts in organization's known for innovative practices.

_____ 68.   Review how dedicated budgets are funded from noted organizations for R&D and innovation.

_____ 69.   Investigate how noted organizations quantify benefits from their innovation efforts.

_____ 70.   Investigate process innovations' impact on mid-sized service firms.

_____ 71.   Investigate amount of sales, profits, or efficiency gains produced by new innovative offerings from noted organizations.

_____ 72.   Review organizational business plans that address innovation.

_____ 73.   Review notable organization's average time-to-profitability in months for new product/service development projects.

_____ 74.   Investigate notable organization's average time in days to market for new products/services.

_____ 75. Review notable organization's percentage of revenue from innovative products launched in the past three years.

_____ 76. Review innovation spending into enhancements to existing products/processes/business models as a percentage of total innovation spending in products/processes/business models.

_____ 77. Review innovation spending into new or white space opportunities (new category of products/processes/business models) as a percentage of total innovation spending in products/processes/business models.

_____ 78. Review innovation spending into products/processes/business models other then enhancements, extensions, or white space opportunities as a percentage of total innovation spending in products/processes/business models.

_____ 79. Investigate various innovative product/service trends of select organizations.

_____ 80. Review best training practices for innovative products/services from a select group of organizations.

_____ 81. Review various cycle-time measures for innovation that are being used by select organizations.

_____ 82. Visit the General Electric (GE) Crotonville Corporate University, in Ossining, New York, was launched in 1956 and is considered the oldest corporate university in the nation. Review their course offerings and learn how their program and course offerings support corporate innovation and GE's employee growth and development corporate-wide.

_____ 83. Review how various organizations define innovation and innovative practices.

_____ 84. Review a select group of service firms and manufacturers who were most successful in launching products/services they had never before offered.

_____ 85. Review the various models of corporate innovation and how innovation is being managed.

_____ 86. Investigate average time for innovative new products/services to break-even.

_____ 87. Review selected organizations results regarding impact of sales results from innovation performance.

_____ 88. Review various organizations innovation growth strategies and implementation.

_____ 89. Review select organizations' use of market intelligence in exploring innovative opportunities for their products/services.

_____ 90. Review various organizations' innovation cross-functional teams.

_____ 91. Review how various organizations launch innovation in relevant markets.

_____ 92. Review various innovation networks.

_____ 93. Investigate how select organizations use strategic networks to source new ideas (e.g. universities, think tanks, and research institutes, etc.).

_____ 94. Review companies who have been driven by visionary innovators (e.g. Apple, Alphabet, etc.).

_____ 95. Review companies who have been driven by strategic innovators (e.g. Berkshire Hathaway).

_____ 96. Investigate "fast follower" companies that master the ability to be the first to deliver innovation to market.

_____ 97. Review various corporate promotions of in-house innovation reward/recognition programs.

_____ 98.   Review various corporate work spaces that promotes innovation within the workforce.

_____ 99.   Review how leading organizations define clear roles and responsibilities for driving innovation.

_____ 100.   Review how innovative organizations foster a creative learning environment within the workplace.

NOTES

Interviewing Hints and Tips

Interviewing Hints and Tips

DO'S

- Be positive when asking questions.

- Allow participants time to formulate answers.

- Make sure questions are understood.

- Reword questions to aid understanding.

- Encourage all participants to answer questions.

- Appear to be interested in all respondents' answers.

- Thank participants for their time.

DON'TS

- Do not ask questions beyond what the criteria are asking.

- Never read more into the answer than is intended by the question.

- Do not ask rhetorical questions.

- Do not disagree with answers.

- Never be repetitious when asking questions.

- Do not make loaded statements when asking questions.

- Do not allow one participant to monopolize all answers.

Corporate Innovation Assessment Interview Plan and Timetable

Planning Sheet – Date _____   Assessment Location: _____

Area Contact Person: _____   Office Phone: _____   Cell Phone: _____

Leadership 8:30 a.m.–9:30 a.m.	Strategic Planning 9:35 a.m.-10:35 a.m.	Customer Focus 10:40 a.m. – 11:40 a.m.	Measurement, Analysis, and Knowledge Mgmt. 11:45 a.m. – 12:45 p.m.	Workforce Focus 12:50 p.m. – 1:50 p.m.	Process Management 1:55 p.m. – 2:55 p.m.	Results 3:00 p.m. – 4:00 p.m.
• Executive Level	• Executive Level	• Executive Level	• Executive Level	• Executive Level	• Executive Level	• Executive Level
NAME ___ Position ___	NAME ___ Position ___	NAME ___ Position ___	NAME ___ Position ___	NAME ___ Position ___	NAME ___ Position ___	NAME ___ Position ___
NAME ___ Position ___	NAME ___ Position ___	NAME ___ Position ___	NAME ___ Position ___	NAME ___ Position ___	NAME ___ Position ___	NAME ___ Position ___
NAME ___ Position ___	NAME ___ Position ___	NAME ___ Position ___	NAME ___ Position ___	NAME ___ Position ___	NAME ___ Position ___	NAME ___ Position ___
• Middle Management	• Middle Management	• Middle Management	• Middle Management	• Middle Management	• Middle Management	• Middle Management
NAME ___ Position ___	NAME ___ Position ___	NAME ___ Position ___	NAME ___ Position ___	NAME ___ Position ___	NAME ___ Position ___	NAME ___ Position ___
NAME ___ Position ___	NAME ___ Position ___	NAME ___ Position ___	NAME ___ Position ___	NAME ___ Position ___	NAME ___ Position ___	NAME ___ Position ___
NAME ___ Position ___	NAME ___ Position ___	NAME ___ Position ___	NAME ___ Position ___	NAME ___ Position ___	NAME ___ Position ___	NAME ___ Position ___
• Frontline Staff	• Frontline Staff	• Frontline Staff	• Frontline Staff	• Frontline Staff	• Frontline Staff	• Frontline Staff
NAME ___ Position ___	NAME ___ Position ___	NAME ___ Position ___	NAME ___ Position ___	NAME ___ Position ___	NAME ___ Position ___	NAME ___ Position ___
NAME ___ Position ___	NAME ___ Position ___	NAME ___ Position ___	NAME ___ Position ___	NAME ___ Position ___	NAME ___ Position ___	NAME ___ Position ___
NAME ___ Position ___	NAME ___ Position ___	NAME ___ Position ___	NAME ___ Position ___	NAME ___ Position ___	NAME ___ Position ___	NAME ___ Position ___

E Corporate Innovation Documentation List

Document Description	Document Date	Revision Date	Document Location	Document Owner

NOTES

F Corporate Innovation (CI) Sustainability Index[31]

Note: Review all Corporate Innovation (CI) initiatives and score % complete and document names and site locations.

Corporate Innovation Initiative Areas		Triple Bottom Line (3BL) Sustainability Dimensions	Corporate Innovation Initiative Sustainability Status	Where to Find Corporate Innovation Initiative (Document Name and Site Location)	Total Points Possible (A)	% Percent Secure 0-100% 10% units (B)	Corporate Innovation Sustainability Index (AxB)=C
1.1 Senior Leadership	Vision, Mission, and Values	Economic	○ ○		70	___ %	
	Legal/ Ethical Behavior	Environmental	○ ○				
	Commitment to Social Issues	Social	○ ○				
1.2 Governance and Societal Responsibilities	Community Investments	Economic	○ ○		50	___ %	
	Environmental Plan	Environmental	○ ○				
	Diversity Plan	Social	○ ○				
2.1 Strategy Development	Financial Plan and Budget	Economic	○ ○		40	___ %	
	Environmental Plan	Environmental	○ ○				
	Human Resource Plan	Social	○ ○				

Corporate Innovation (CI) Sustainability Index

Note: Review all Corporate Innovation (CI) initiatives and score % complete and document names and site locations.

CI Sustainability Legend
Complete Initiative: ●●
Partial Initiative: ●○
No Initiative: ○○

Corporate Innovation Initiative Areas	Corporate Innovation Initiative Areas	Triple Bottom Line (3BL) Sustainability Dimensions	Corporate Innovation Initiative Sustainability Status	Where to Find Corporate Innovation Initiative (Document Name and Site Location)	Total Points Possible (A)	% Percent Secure 0-100% 10% units (B)	Corporate Innovation Sustainability Index (AxB)=C
2.2 Strategy Deployment	Economic Action Plans	Economic	○○		45	____%	
	Environmental Action Plans	Environmental	○○				
	Social Issues Action Plans	Social	○○				
3.1 Customer Engagement	Market Analysis	Economic	○○		40	____%	
	Environmental Issues Identified for Customers	Environmental	○○				
	Customer Concerns Addressed	Social	○○				
3.2 Voice of the Customer	Customer Engagement	Economic	○○		45	____%	
	Environmental Planning	Environmental	○○				
	Customer Issues Surveyed/Analyzed	Social	○○				
4.1 Measurement, Analysis, and Improvement of Organizational Performance	Financial Performance Data	Economic	○○		45	____%	
	Environmental Data	Environmental	○○				
	Workforce Performance Data	Social	○○				

Corporate Innovation (CI) Sustainability Index

Note: Review all Corporate Innovation (CI) initiatives and score % complete and document names and site locations.

CI Sustainability Legend

Complete Initiative:	● ●
Partial Initiative:	● ○
No Initiative:	○ ○

Corporate Innovation Initiative Areas	Corporate Innovation Initiative	Triple Bottom Line (3BL) Sustainability Dimensions	Corporate Innovation Initiative Sustainability Status	Where to Find Corporate Innovation Initiative (Document Name and Site Location)	Total Points Possible (A)	% Percent Secure 0-100% 10% units (B)	Corporate Innovation Sustainability Index (A×B)=C
4.2 Management of Information, Knowledge, and Information Technology	Risk Management Data	Economic	○ ○		45	___ %	
	Conservation/ Recycling Data	Environmental	○ ○				
	"Best Practice" Knowledge/ Benchmark Data	Social	○ ○				
5.1 Workforce Engagement	Productivity Plans	Economic	○ ○		45	___ %	
	Ethical Practices Addressed	Environmental	○ ○				
	Training & Development	Social	○ ○				
5.2 Workforce Environment	Succession Planning	Economic	○ ○		40	___ %	
	Workforce Environmental Factors Addressed	Environmental	○ ○				
	Cultural Diversity Addressed	Social	○ ○				
6.1 Work Systems	Work Systems Review(s)	Economic	○ ○		35	___ %	
	Emergency Readiness Plan	Environmental	○ ○				
	Work Systems Re-engineering Efforts Documented	Social	○ ○				

Corporate Innovation (CI) Sustainability Index

Note: Review all Corporate Innovation (CI) initiatives and score % complete and document names and site locations.

CI Sustainability Legend

Complete Initiative:	●●
Partial Initiative:	●○
No Initiative:	○○

Corporate Innovation Initiative Areas	Corporate Innovation Initiative Areas	Triple Bottom Line (3BL) Sustainability Dimensions	Corporate Innovation Initiative Sustainability Status	Where to Find Corporate Innovation Initiative (Document Name and Site Location)	Total Points Possible (A)	% Percent Secure 0-100% 10% units (B)	Corporate Innovation Sustainability Index (AxB)=C
6.2 Work Processes	Work Systems Design	Economic	○○				
	Environmental Purchasing Plan	Environmental	○○		50	___%	
	Workflow Analysis	Social	○○				
7.1 Educational Program/SVS Outcomes	Market Results	Economic	○○				
	Customer/Supplier Results	Environmental	○○		100	___%	
	Corporate Results	Social	○○				
7.2 Customer-focused Outcomes	Customer Satisfaction Results	Economic	○○				
	Environmental Policy Change Results	Environmental	○○		70	___%	
	Industry Benchmark Results	Social	○○				
7.3 Financial and Market Outcomes	Dashboard Indicators	Economic	○○				
	Risk Management Results	Environmental	○○		70	___%	
	Financial/ Market Trends	Social	○○				

Corporate Innovation (CI) Sustainability Index

Note: Review all Corporate Innovation (CI) initiatives and score % complete and document names and site locations.

CI Sustainability Legend
Complete Initiative: ●●
Partial Initiative: ●○
No Initiative: ○○

	Corporate Innovation Initiative Areas	Triple Bottom Line (3BL) Sustainability Dimensions	Corporate Innovation Initiative Sustainability Status	Where to Find Corporate Innovation Initiative (Document Name and Site Location)	Total Points Possible (A)	% Percent Secure 0-100% 10% units (B)	Corporate Innovation Sustainability Index (AxB)=C
7.4 Workforce-focused Outcomes	Staff and Leader Development Results	Economic	○○				
	Training and Safety Results	Environmental	○○		70	____ %	
	Workforce Climate Results	Social	○○				
7.5 Process Effectiveness Outcomes	Productivity Results	Economic	○○				
	Business Continuity/Preparedness Results	Environmental	○○		70	____ %	
	Process Innovation Results	Social	○○				
7.6 Leadership Outcomes	Community Support Results	Economic	○○				
	Environmental Results	Environmental	○○		70	____ %	
	Corporate Governance Results	Social	○○				

TOTAL INDEX POINTS 1,000

_____ **Sustainability Index**

Index Score Profiles

Corporate Innovation (CI) Sustainability Index

Range	Common Characteristics
DISTRIBUTION OF SCORES	
0-125	Very early stages of developing approaches to addressing some basic corporate innovation initiative planning and integration issues.
126-250	Early stages in the implementation of approaches. Important gaps exist in most categories for corporate innovation initiative planning, integration and implementation.
251-400	Beginning of a systematic approach, but major gaps exist in approach and deployment in some categories. Early stages of obtaining results stemming from approaches in corporate innovation initiative planning, integration and implementation.
401-600	Effective approaches and good results in most categories, but deployment in some key areas is still too early to demonstrate results. Further deployment measures and results are needed to demonstrate integration, continuity, and maturity in corporate innovation initiative planning and implementation.
601-750	Refined approaches, including key measures, good deployment and good results in most categories. Some outstanding activities and results clearly demonstrated. Good evidence of continuity and maturity in key areas. Basis of further deployment and integration is in place. May be an industry leader in corporate innovation initiative planning, and implementation.
751-875	Refined approaches, excellent deployment, and good to excellent improvement levels demonstrated in all categories, good to excellent integration. Industry leaders and a national model in corporate innovation initiative planning.
875-1000	Outstanding approaches, full deployment, excellent and sustained results. Excellent integration. National and world leadership in corporate innovation initiative planning and implementation.

Note: The above Corporate Innovation (CI) Sustainability Index score ranges can be used to gauge an organization's overall progress and maturity in corporate innovation initiative planning, integration and implementation. The Corporate Innovation (CI) Sustainability Index is based on the Global Reporting Initiative (GRI) Triple Bottom Line (Economic – Environmental - Social) framework.

Corporate Innovation Plan and Budget
(Based on assessment results)

Worksheet (Sample)

XYZ organization
(name of organization)

VISION STATEMENT

XYZ Organization will be a global leader in producing and providing innovative products and services.

MISSION STATEMENT

To provide state-of-the-art innovative products and services to our customers.

SHARED VALUES

(1) Sharing of "Best Practice" knowledge throughout the workplace

(2) Environment that supports innovative practices and entrepreneurship

(3) Mutual respect for knowledge among all employee levels

(4) Respect the use of technology to help transfer knowledge throughout the workforce

(5) View employee creativity as a competitiveness issue for the organization

Leadership

Objective #1: Expand leadership involvement in corporate innovation planning.

Strategic Planning

Objective #2: Develop a strategic Corporate Innovation Plan.

Customer Focus

Objective #3: Align corporate innovation initiatives with key customers and markets.

Measurement, Analysis, & Knowledge Management

Objective #4: Collect key measures, analyze, and transfer corporate innovation "Best Practices" data and information.

Workforce Focus

Objective #5: Define roles and responsibilities and include updated information in Job Descriptions for employees involved in corporate innovation initiatives.

Process Management

Objective #6: Flowchart and document key corporate innovation processes/practices.

Results

Objective #7: Collect and share with suppliers, partners, customers, and employees key corporate innovation results data.

Note: This document is completed after the organizational assessment for corporate innovation has been conducted.

Corporate Innovation Plan and Budget

Worksheet (Sample)

Leadership

Objective #1: Expand leadership involvement in corporate innovation planning.

Strategies	Costs
1A – Senior leadership to develop a Corporate Innovation Plan.	$1,000
1B – Senior leadership to develop a personal leadership plan to promote corporate innovation training throughout the organization.	$1,000
1C – Managers and supervisors to be held accountable for meeting the organization's strategic plans and goals for corporate innovation.	$ 500
1D – Senior leadership to increase involvement in key supplier, partner, and customer in corporate innovation training/development initiatives.	$2,000
TOTAL COSTS	**$4,500**

Corporate Innovation Plan and Budget

Worksheet (Sample)

Strategic Planning

Objective #2: Develop a strategic Corporate Innovation Plan.

Strategies	Costs
2A – Involve employees, suppliers, partners, and customers in the organization's strategic planning process for corporate innovation.	$1,500
2B – Develop a recognition budget for corporate innovation.	$5,000
2C – Benchmark other leading organizations' corporate innovation initiatives and use findings to develop the Corporate Innovation Plan.	$4,000
TOTAL COSTS	$10,500

Corporate Innovation Plan and Budget

Worksheet (Sample)

Customer Focus

Objective #3: Align corporate innovation initiatives with key customers and markets.

Strategies	**Costs**
3A – Survey key customers annually regarding innovative opportunities that need to be addressed.	$4,000
3B – Benchmark organizations that provide value-added corporate innovation initiatives to their customers.	$4,000
3C – Review leading innovative industry initiatives that are being offered.	$2,000
3D – Provide key customers value-added innovative products/services.	$8,000
TOTAL COSTS	$18,000

Corporate Innovation Plan and Budget

Worksheet (Sample)

Measurement, Analysis, and Knowledge Management

Objective #4: Collect key measures, analyze, and transfer corporate innovation "Best Practice"

data and information.

Strategies	Costs
4A – Aggregate and track "Bests Practice" corporate innovation data/information.	$2,000
4B – Involve employees at all levels in analyzing key corporate innovation data and information.	$6,000
4C – Collect, document, and transfer "Best Practice" corporate innovation knowledge throughout the organization.	$3,000
4D – Ensure that all corporate innovation data and information is user-friendly, timely, and relevant.	$2,000
TOTAL COSTS	$13,000

Corporate Innovation Plan and Budget

Worksheet (Sample)

Workforce Focus

Objective #5: <u>Define roles and responsibilities and include updated information in Job</u> <u>Descriptions for employees involved in corporate innovation initiatives.</u>

Strategies	**Costs**
5A – Identify Subject Matter Experts (SME's) in key corporate innovation processes throughout the organization.	$1,000
5B – Develop roles and responsibilities for employees involved in corporate innovation initiatives within the organization.	$1,000
5C – Develop a corporate innovation mentoring program.	$3,000
5D – Develop a consistent follow-up procedure to ensure that all corporate innovation knowledge received in training has on-the-job application.	$2,000
TOTAL COSTS	$7,000

Corporate Innovation Plan and Budget

Worksheet (Sample)

Process Management

Objective #6: Flowchart and document key corporate innovation processes/practices.

Strategies	Costs
6A – Incorporate problem-solving tools to evaluate, improve, and identify corporate innovation process upsets and problems.	$4,000
6B – Identify eight to 12 corporate measurement indicators to gauge on-going process improvement for corporate innovation.	$1,000
6C – Document key corporate innovation processes to ensure consistency throughout the organization.	$3,000
TOTAL COSTS	$8,000

Corporate Innovation Plan and Budget

Worksheet (Sample)

Results

Objective #7: <u>Collect and share with suppliers, partners, customers, and employees key corporate innovation results data.</u>

Strategies	**Costs**
7A – Collect, trend, and deploy key corporate innovation results throughout the organization.	$1,000
7B – Collect and trend employee project results for corporate innovation.	$1,000
7C – Collect results and trends of key vendors, partners, and customers involvement in corporate innovation initiatives.	$1,000
7D – Collect reliable corporate innovation performance data on key competitors.	$1,000
TOTAL COSTS	$4,000
Total Corporate Innovation Costs:	$65,000

— SAMPLE —
STRATEGIC PLANNING WORSHEEET FOR A CORPORATE INNOVATION PLAN

Category (circle one)

1 Leadership

2 Strategic Planning

3 Customer Focus

4 Measurement, Analysis and Knowledge
 Management

5 Workforce Focus

6 Process Management

7 Results

Term (circle one)

Short term: one to two years

Long term: more than two years

Strategy 1A: Senior leadership to develop a Corporate Innovation Plan

$1,000

ACTION ITEMS (Steps to accomplish strategy)	WHO IS RESPONSIBLE	REVIEW DATE	COMPLETION DATE
1. Define corporate innovation issues and vulnerabilities.	President	January 10	February 28
2. Form a senior management team to review corporate innovation issues.	Vice President	February 5	March 15
3. Cross-functional employee team to develop plan.	Director	March 30	April 10
4. Senior staff finalizes Corporate Innovation Plan.	President and Vice Presidents	April 15	May 15
5. Distribute plan to employees, suppliers, customers, and partners.	Managers	May 29	June 29
6.			
7.			
8.			
9.			
10.			

List action items
in respective order

List individual
responsibilities by
names or position

List review
dates

List completion
dates

Note: Making additional copies of this form is allowed.

Corporate Innovation Plan and Budget
(Based on assessment results)

Worksheet

_____
(name of organization)

VISION STATEMENT

MISSION STATEMENT

SHARED VALUES

Leadership
Objective #1:_____

Strategic Planning
Objective #2:_____

Customer Focus
Objective #3:_____

Measurement, Analysis, & Knowledge Management
Objective #4:_____

Workforce Focus
Objective #5:_____

Process Management
Objective #6:_____

Results
Objective #7:_____

Note: This document is completed after the organizational Assessment for Innovation has been conducted.

Corporate Innovation Plan and Budget

Worksheet

Leadership

Objective #1:_____

Strategies	Costs
1A	$
1B	$
1C	$
1D	$
1E	$
1F	$
1G	$
TOTAL COSTS	**$**

Strategic Planning

Objective #2:_____

Strategies	Costs
2A	$
2B	$
2C	$
2D	$
2E	$
2F	$
2G	$
TOTAL COSTS	**$**

Corporate Innovation Plan and Budget

Worksheet

Customer Focus

Objective #3:_____

	Strategies	Costs
3A		$
3B		$
3C		$
3D		$
3E		$
3F		$
3G		$
	TOTAL COSTS	**$**

Measurement, Analysis, and Knowledge Management

Objective #4:_____

	Strategies	Costs
4A		$
4B		$
4C		$
4D		$
4E		$
4F		$
4G		$
	TOTAL COSTS	**$**

Corporate Innovation Plan and Budget

Worksheet

Workforce Focus
Objective #5:_____

	Strategies	Costs
5A		$
5B		$
5C		$
5D		$
5E		$
5F		$
5G		$
	TOTAL COSTS	**$**

Process Management
Objective #6:_____

	Strategies	Costs
6A		$
6B		$
6C		$
6D		$
6E		$
6F		$
6G		$
	TOTAL COSTS	**$**

Corporate Innovation Plan and Budget

Worksheet

Results

Objective #7:_____

	Strategies	Costs
7A		$
7B		$
7C		$
7D		$
7E		$
7F		$
7G		$
	TOTAL COSTS	**$**

Total Corporate Innovation Plan Costs: $

STRATEGIC PLANNING WORKSHEET FOR A CORPORATE INNOVATION PLAN

Category (circle one)

1 Leadership

2 Strategic Planning

3 Customer Focus

4 Measurement, Analysis and Knowledge
  Management

5 Workforce Focus

6 Process Management

7 Results

Term (circle one)

Short term: one to two years

Long term: more than two years

Strategy: _____ $ _____

ACTION ITEMS (Steps to accomplish strategy)	WHO IS RESPONSIBLE	REVIEW DATE	COMPLETION DATE
1.			
2.			
3.			
4.			
5.			
6.			
7.			
8.			
9.			
10.			

Note: Making additional copies of this form is allowed.

H Glossaries of Performance Excellence and Corporate Innovation Terms

Performance Excellence Assessment Terms [32]

Action Plans: Refers to specific actions that respond to short- and longer-term strategic objectives.

Administrative processes and support services: processes and services that may include activities and operations such as finance and accounting, software services, marketing, public relations, information services, purchasing, personnel, legal services, facilities management, research and development, secretarial, and other administrative services.

Alignment: Refers to consistency of plans, processes, information, resource decisions, actions, results, and analyses to support key organization-wide goals.

Analysis: Refers to an examination of facts and data to provide a basis for effective decisions. Analysis often involves the determination of cause-effect relationships.

Anecdotal: Refers to process information that lacks specific methods, measures, deployment mechanisms, and evaluation, improvement, and learning factors. Anecdotal information frequently uses examples and describes individual activities rather than systematic processes.

Approach: Refers to the methods used by an organization to address the Baldrige Criteria Item requirements. Approach includes the appropriateness of the methods to the Item requirements and the effectiveness of their use.

Baldrige Criteria for Performance Excellence: Refers to the associated award that was established by the Malcolm Baldrige National Quality Improvement Act of 1987 (Public Law 100–107). The program and award were named for Malcolm Baldrige, who served as United States Secretary of Commerce during the Reagan administration, from 1981 until Baldrige's 1987 death in a rodeo accident. In 2010, the program's name was changed to the Baldrige Performance Excellence Program to reflect the evolution of the field of quality from a focus on product, service, and customer quality to a broader, strategic focus on overall organizational quality—called performance excellence. The award promotes awareness of performance excellence as an increasingly important element in competitiveness. It also promotes the sharing of successful performance strategies and the benefits derived from using these strategies. To receive a Baldrige Award, an organization must have a role-model organizational management system that ensures continuous improvement in delivering products and/or services, demonstrates efficient and effective operations, and provides a way of engaging and responding to customers and other stakeholders. The award is not given for specific products or services.

Baldrige Assessment: an organizational evaluation based on the seven Baldrige Criteria for Performance Excellence categories, which include, 1. Leadership, 2. Strategic Planning, 3. Customer Focus, 4. Measurement, Analysis, and Knowledge Management, 5. Workforce Focus, 6. Process Management, and 7. Results.

Basic Requirements: Refers to the topic Criteria users need to address when responding to the most central concept of an Item.

Benchmarking: teams of employees review and visit best practice programs, services, and practices. Benchmarking can include site visits to other organizations and telephone interviews. Benchmarking is an involved process that organizations pursue when seeking to become "world- class" in processes that they have identified as needing improvement.

Business and Support Services: includes units and operations involving finance and accounting, software services, sales, marketing, public relations, information services, purchasing and personnel, and so forth.

Business Ethics: a published statement of values and business ethics that are promoted and practiced both internally and externally by the organization.

Business Plan: a statement of business objectives and strategies that is published and shared throughout an organization. Many organizations, when beginning their quality improvement process, have a separate business and quality plans.

Collaborators: Refers to those organizations or individuals who cooperate with an organization to support a particular activity or event or who cooperate on an intermittent basis when short-term goals are aligned or are the same. Typically, collaborations do not involve formal agreements or arrangements.

Competitive Comparisons: an organization's comparison of its products/ services against major competitors and industry comparisons.

Control Chart: a graph that is used by employees to determine if their work process is within prescribed limits.

Core Competencies: Refers to an organization's areas of greatest expertise.

Cross- functional Teams: teams formed from different divisions or departments to solve or create new solutions to an organizational problem or opportunity.

Customer: the end- user of all products and services produced within an organization. Customers are both internal and external.

Customer Contact Employee: an employee who has direct interface with external customers, in person, via telephone, or other means.

Customer Relationship Management: an organization's interactions and relationships with its customers.

Cycle Time: the amount of time it takes to complete a specified work process.

Data: the collection of facts, information, or statistics.

Data Analysis: the breaking apart of data to help the organization gauge improvement.

Deployment: Refers to the *extent* to which an approach is applied in addressing the requirements of a Baldrige Criteria Item. Deployment is evaluated on the basis of the breadth and depth of application of the approach to relevant work units throughout the organization.

Diversity: Refers to valuing and benefiting from personal differences. These differences address many variables, including race, religion, color, gender, national origin, disability, sexual orientation, age and generational preferences, education, geographic origin, and skill characteristics, as well as differences in ideas, thinking, academic disciplines, and perspectives.

Documented Improvement: a process improvement that has been supported against baseline data and documented at measured intervals.

Effective: Refers to how well a process or a measure addresses its intended purpose. Determining effectiveness requires (1) the evaluation of how well the process is aligned with the organization's needs and how well the process is deployed or (2) the evaluation of the outcome of the measure used.

Employee Involvement: involvement of employees across the organization at all levels.

Employee Morale: the attitudes of employees in regard to their willingness to perform work tasks.

Empowerment: employees' freedom to respond to customer demands and requests.

Ergonomics: the evaluation of an organization's facilities and equipment to ensure compatibility between workers and their work processes.

Ethical Behavior: Refers to how an organization ensures that all its decisions, actions, and stakeholder interactions conform to the organization's moral and professional principles.

Flowchart: a graphic map of a work process used by employee teams to document the current condition of a process.

Goals and Strategies: organizations develop goals and strategies for short-term (1 to 2 years) and long-term (2 years or more) desired results. Goals and strategies are usually written and distributed across the organization.

Governance: Refers to the system of management and controls exercised in the stewardship of an organization. It includes the responsibilities of an organization's owners/shareholders, board of directors, and senior leaders.

High-Performance Work: Refers to work processes used to systematically pursue ever-higher levels of overall organizational and individual performance, including quality, productivity, innovation rate, and cycle time performance. High-performance work results in improved service for customers and other stakeholders.

Improvement Plan: a written plan that the organization has published to accomplish desired improvement results.

Innovation: Refers to making meaningful change to improve products, processes, or organizational effectiveness and to create new value for stakeholders. Innovation involves the adoption of an idea, process, technology, product, or business model that is either new or new to its proposed application.

Integration: Refers to the harmonization of plans, processes, information, resource decisions, actions, results, and analyses to support key organization-wide goals. Effective integration goes beyond alignment and is achieved when the individual components of a performance management system operate as a fully interconnected unit.

Internal Customer/ Supplier Network: an organization's employee network; referred to as inside customers and suppliers.

Key: Refers to the major or most important elements or factors, those that are critical to achieving an intended outcome.

Key Indicators: key measures of performance (i.e., productivity, cycle time, cost, and other effectiveness measures).

Knowledge Assets: Refers to the accumulated intellectual resources of an organization. It is the knowledge possessed by the organization and its workforce in the form of information, ideas, learning, understanding, memory, insights, cognitive and technical skills, and capabilities. The workforce, software, patents, databases, documents, guides, policies and procedures, and technical drawings are repositories of an organization's knowledge assets. Knowledge assets are held not only by an organization but reside within its customers, suppliers, and partners as well.

Leadership System: Refers to how leadership is exercised, formally and informally, throughout the organization; it is the basis for and the way key decisions are made, communicated, and carried out.

Learning: Refers to new knowledge or skills acquired through evaluation, study, experience, and innovation.

Levels: Refers to numerical information that places or positions an organization's results and performance on a meaningful measurement scale. Performance levels permit evaluation relative to past performance, projections, goals, and appropriate comparisons.

Manufacturing Organization: an organization that makes or processes raw materials into a finished product.

Measurement: the process of gauging an organization's results against its customer requirements.

Measures and Indicators: Refers to numerical information that quantifies input, output, and performance dimensions of processes, products, programs, projects, services, and the overall organization (outcomes). Measures and indicators might be simple (derived from one measurement) or composite.

Mission: Refers to the overall function of an organization. The mission answers the question, "What is this organization attempting to accomplish?" The mission might define customers or markets served, distinctive or core competencies, or technologies used.

Mission Statement: many organizations have a published document that defines its reason for existing. The mission statement is shared with employees, suppliers, and customers.

Partners: Refers to those key organizations or individuals who are working in concert with an organization to achieve a common goal or to improve performance. Typically, partnerships are formal arrangements for a specific aim or purpose, such as to achieve a strategic objective or to deliver a specific product or service.

Performance: Refers to outputs and their outcomes obtained from processes, products, and customers that permit evaluation and comparison relative to goals, standards, past results, and other organizations. Performance can be expressed in nonfinancial and financial terms.

Performance Data: results of improvements in product and service production and delivery processes.

Performance Excellence: Refers to an integrated approach to organizational performance management that results in (1) delivery of ever-improving value to customers and stakeholders, contributing to organizational sustainability; (2) improvement of overall organizational effectiveness and capabilities; and (3) organizational and personal learning.

Performance Projections: Refers to estimates of future performance. Projections may be inferred from past performance, may be based on competitors' or similar organizations' performance that must be met or exceeded, may be predicted based on changes in a dynamic environment, or may be goals for future performance.

Process: a series of steps linked together to provide a product or service for an end user.

Process Control: a control device to detect and remove causes of variation to a defined process.

Process Management: organization's maintenance of defined processes to ensure that both quality and performance are continuously improved.

Productivity: Refers to measures of the efficiency of resource use.

Productivity Improvement: measured reduction in an organization's key operational processes.

Problem-solving Tools: tools used by teams to solve process problems (i.e., flowcharts, Pareto analysis, histograms, control charts, cause-and-effect diagrams, and matrix diagrams).

Problem-solving Teams: teams of employees selected and empowered by management to assess, analyze, and solve problems within an organization. These teams may be cross-functional, work group, departmental, or project-focused.

Public Responsibility: an organization's impact and possible impact on society with its products, services, and operations. This includes business ethics, environment, education, health care, community services, and safety as they relate to the public.

Quality Plan: a written statement of an organization's plan for maintaining and improving quality. An organization that has just begun the quality improvement process usually has this plan separate from its business plan. A mature organization usually integrates its quality plan with the business plan.

Quality Results: an organization's achievement levels and improvement trends.

Results: Refers to outputs and outcomes achieved by an organization.

Safe Work Practices: an organization's promotion of safety on the worksite for employees. Many organizations have documented guidelines for employees to follow, and they collect data on safe work practices.

Senior Executive: refers to the organization's highest- ranking official and those reporting directly to that official.

Senior Leaders: Refers to an organization's senior management group or team.

Service Organization: non- manufacturing organizations, such as utilities, schools, government, transportation, finance, real estate, restaurants, hotels, news media, business services, professional services, and repair services.

Small Business: complete businesses with no more than 500 full- time employees. Business activities may include manufacturing and/or service.

Stakeholders: Refers to all groups that are or might be affected by an organization's actions and success. Examples of key stakeholders might include customers, the workforce, partners, collaborators, governing boards, stockholders, donors, suppliers, taxpayers, regulatory bodies, policy makers, funders, and local and professional communities.

Statistical Process Control (SPC): technique for measuring and analyzing process variations.

Strategic Advantages: Refers to those marketplace benefits that exert a decisive influence on an organization's likelihood of future success.

Strategic Challenges: Refers to those pressures that exert a decisive influence on an organization's likelihood of future success.

Strategic Objectives: Refers to an organization's articulated aims or responses to address major change or improvement, competitiveness or social issues, and business advantages.

Strategic Plan: a detailed plan of action developed by an organization establishing and defining measurable goals to achieve continuous quality improvement within the organization. A strategic plan can be broken into short term (1 to 2 years) and long term (more than 2 years).

Supplier: an individual or group, either internal to the organization or external, that provides input to a work group or customer.

Supplier Certification Program: a formal supplier program used by an organization to improve supplier quality. Many organizations partner with critical suppliers and establish a relationship of trust and measurable results.

Supplier Partnership: a supplier process practiced by many service and manufacturing organizations. Organizations establish a preferred supplier program that is based on a trust relationship with measurable results. Supplier partnerships are usually a prelude to a more formalized supplier certification program.

Survey Process: the means by which an organization collects data from its customers and employees. These surveys may help an organization focus on internal/external customer satisfaction issues.

Sustainability: Refers to an organization's ability to address current business needs and to have the agility and strategic management to prepare successfully for future business, market, and operating environment. Sustainability considerations might include workforce capability and capacity, resource availability, technology, knowledge, core competencies, work systems, facilities, and equipment. Sustainability might be affected by changes in the marketplace and customer preferences, changes in the financial markets, and changes in the legal and regulatory environment. In addition, sustainability has a component related to day-to-day preparedness for real-time or short-term emergencies.

System: a set of well-defined and well-designed processes for meeting the organization's quality and performance requirements.

Systematic: Refers to approaches that are well-ordered, are repeatable, and use data and information so learning is possible. In other words, approaches are systematic if they build in the opportunity for evaluation, improvement, and sharing, thereby permitting a gain in maturity.

Targets: desired goals that organizations have in their strategic planning processes.

Third-party Survey: a survey conducted by a resource outside the organization.

Total Quality Management (TQM): a management philosophy that focuses on continuous quality improvement throughout an organization.

Trends: Refers to numerical information that shows the direction and rate of change for an organization's results. Trends provide a time sequence of organizational performance. A minimum of three historical (not projected) data points generally are needed to begin to ascertain a trend. More data points are needed to define a statistically valid trend. The time period for a trend is determined by the cycle time of the process being measured

User-friendly: a process that is understandable to all levels of a workforce within an organization. A user-friendly process can be understood because it is written in simpler, more understandable language.

Values Statement: a published document that describes an organization's beliefs. This values statement is usually shared with faculty, staff, students, customers, suppliers, and the community.

Vision: Refers to the desired future state of an organization. The vision describes where the organization is headed, what it intends to be, or how it wishes to be perceived in the future.

Vision Statement: many organizations have a published document that defines their direction for the next 5 to 10 years. The vision statement is shared with both internal and external groups.

Work Processes: Refers to an organization's most important internal value creation processes. They might include product design and delivery, customer support, supply chain management, business, and support processes. They are the processes that involve the majority of an organization's workforce and produce customer, stakeholder, and stockholder value. Key work processes frequently relate to core competencies, to the factors that determine success relative to competitors, and to the factors considered important for business growth by senior leaders.

Work Systems: Refers to how the work of an organization is accomplished. Work systems involve the workforce, key suppliers and partners, contractors, collaborators, and other components of the supply chain needed to produce and deliver products. It also refers to business and support processes.

Workforce: Refers to all people actively involved in accomplishing the work of an organization, including paid employees (e.g., permanent, part-time, temporary, and telecommuting employees, as well as contract employees supervised by the organization) and volunteers, as appropriate. The workforce includes team leaders, supervisors, and managers at all levels.

Workforce Capability: Refers to an organization's ability to accomplish its work processes through the knowledge, skills, abilities, and competencies of its people.

Workforce Capacity: Refers to an organization's ability to ensure sufficient staffing levels to accomplish its work processes and successfully deliver products to customers, including the ability to meet seasonal or varying demand levels.

Workforce Engagement: Refers to the extent of workforce commitment, emotional and intellectual, to accomplishing the work, mission, and vision of the organization. Organizations with high levels of workforce engagement are often characterized by high-performing work environments in which people are motivated to do their utmost for the benefit of their customers and for the success of the organization.

World-class Organization: an organization that produces excellent results in major areas with a sound quality management approach to corporate innovation. This organization is totally integrated with a systematic prevention-based system that is continuously refined through evaluations and improvement cycles.

Zero-based Organization: an organization that has no system in place for corporate innovation and is anecdotal in its implementation of a sound, systematic, effective, and management-based approach to corporate innovation that is fully integrated and implemented across the organization.

Innovation Terms [33]

Applied research: Original investigation undertaken in order to acquire new knowledge directed primarily towards a specific practical aim or objective. Can include prototypes and pilot plant.

Accidental Discovery / Invention: An accidental discovery is a law that was discovered due to an accident. An accidental invention is an innovative product its author didn't actually intend toinvent.

Basic research: Experimental or theoretical work undertaken primarily to acquire new knowledge of the underlying foundation of phenomena and observable facts, without any particular application or use in view.

Beta Testing: Beta testing of a new-to-the-world product includes a limited group of users outside of the company. The twin aims of the Beta test are to do a sanity test and to get customer feedback on how the product is used and works in the real world.

Big Data: A term for data sets that are so large or complex that traditional data processing applications are inadequate. Challenges include analysis, capture, data curation, search, sharing, storage, transfer, visualization, querying and information privacy. The term often refers simply to the use of predictive analytics or certain other advanced methods to extract value from data, and seldom to a particular size of data set. Accuracy in big data may lead to more confident decision making, and better decisions can result in greater operational efficiency, cost reduction, and reduced risk.

Brainstorming: Brainstorming is a group session where employees contribute their ideas for solving a problem or meeting a company objective without fear or retribution or ridicule.

Break-even Point: The point at which revenues exceed expenses.

Bridge Financing: A short-term loan made in expectation of intermediate-term or long-term financing. Can be used when a company plans to go public in the near future.

Business Model: Business model converts innovation to economic value for the business and conceptualizes the value proposition that distinguishes a firm from its competitors. It draws on a multitude of business subjects including entrepreneurship, strategy, economics, finance, operations, and marketing, and spells-out how a company generates revenue.

Commercialisation: The process of taking a product or process form early to commercial deployment.

Commercial demonstration: A demonstration, conducted following technology demonstration, aimed at proving that a product or process could proceed to commercial deployment.

Commercial deployment: The condition under which a product or process can be profitably deployed by commercial enterprises regardless of whether public subsidies are involved

Creativity: Creativity is an act of making something new. It is a mental and social process involving the generation of new ideas or concepts, or new associations of the creative mind between existing ideas or concepts.

Creative Process: A sequence of activities that are designed to generate creative thinking.

Demand pull: Demand pull refers to market environments or emerging needs which incentivise innovative products or processes. It can refer either to emerging market opportunities or public sector policies and measures, including subsidies, designed to promote innovation. It is often linked to or used in dichotomy with technology push.

Demonstration: An activity that demonstrates the viability of a product or process

Deployment: The use of a product or process for practical and/or commercial purposes.

Development: Systematic work, drawing on existing knowledge gained from research and/or practical experience, which is directed to producing new materials, products or devices, to installing new processes, systems and services, or to improving substantially those already produced or installed

Derivative Innovation: A secondary product or service derived from a platform innovation. These innovations are slight modifications of the main product

Diffusion: Widespread uptake of a product or process throughout the market of potential adopters

Early deployment: The early use of a product or process for practical and/or commercial purposes. Corresponds roughly to an innovation.

Entrepreneurial Creativity: Coming up with innovative ideas and turning them into value-creating profitable business activities.

Experimental development: See development

Feedback R&D: R&D conducted to solve scientific or technical problems that arise when a product or process is being demonstrated or deployed

Full-scale deployment: Commercial deployment where a product or process has established a new market or has gained a material share of an existing market.

Gazzeles: Publicly traded companies that have grown at least 20% for each of the last four years, starting with at least US$ 1 million in sales.

Incremental innovation: An improvement in performance, cost, reliability, design etc. to an existing commercial product or process without any fundamental novelty in end-use service provision

Innoball: Strategic simulation game "Innovation Football" that helps improve the business model and business strategies of an innovation project, train and evaluate the strength of the innovation team, and make investment decision.

Innovation: New products and processes and significant technological improvements in products and processes. An innovation has taken place if it has been introduced on the market (product innovation) or used within a production process (process innovation). Depending on context, products and processes can be new or improved anywhere in the world, or new or improved in relation to a firm, a market or a country.

Innovation system: The system of actors, institutions, networks and processes that result in innovation taking place. Covers research, development, demonstration and commercial activities leading to deployment. Can be used in reference to countries, sectors or technologies. Formally, covers processes that lead to early deployment but can also be used in an extended sense to include processes leading to commercial or full-scale deployment

Intellectual Property: Any idea or work that can be considered proprietary in nature and is thus protected from infringement by others.

Invention: A new scientific or technical idea, and the means of its embodiment or accomplishment. To be patentable, an invention must be novel, have utility, and be non-obvious.

Market formation: Activities designed to create, enhance, or exploit niche markets and the early commercialisation of technologies in wider markets

Market Window: The interval of time during which a particular type of product can be profitably sold.

Mockup: In manufacturing and design, a mockup, or mock-up, is a scale or full-size model of a design or device, used for teaching, demonstration, design evaluation, promotion, and other purposes. A mockup is called a prototype if it provides at least part of the functionality of a system and enables testing of a design.

Niche markets: Application of a product or process in a limited market setting (or niche) based on a specific relative performance advantage (or on public policy incentives) and typically not exposed to full market competition

Pilot plants: Plant constructed with the principal purposes of obtaining experience and compiling engineering and other data

Platform Innovation: Innovation that leads to the practical application of fundamental innovations and, often, to creation of a new industry. From a business perspective, platform innovation is about seeking out extensions to the current business and leading changes of significant impact.

Prototype: An original model constructed to include all the technical characteristics and performances of a new product or process

Radical innovation: A new product or process that strongly deviates from prevailing norms and so often entails a disruptive change over existing commercial technologies and associated institutions

Research: Creative work undertaken on a systematic basis in order to increase the stock of knowledge, including knowledge of man, culture and society

Research and development (R&D): Creative work undertaken on a systematic basis in order to increase the stock of knowledge, including knowledge of man, culture and society, and the use of this stock of knowledge to devise new applications.

Research, development and demonstration (RD&D): Collective term covering all three activities

Serendipity: An attitude and aptitude for making unintended discoveries by accident.

Start-up: A new business, at the earliest stages of development and financing.

Synergy Innovation: Innovation focused on building innovative synergies.

Technology demonstration: Prototype, rough example or an otherwise incomplete version of a conceivable product or future system, put together as proof of concept with the primary purpose of showcasing the possible applications

Technology push: Technology push is the process of pushing a technology on to the market through RD&D or production and sales functions. It can refer either to firm activities or to public sector policies and measures designed to promote innovation. It is often linked to or used in dichotomy with demand pull.

Technology readiness level (TRL): A type of measurement system developed by NASA to assess the maturity level of a particular technology. Used mainly to assess the readiness of individual technological components to operate in a larger technology system. Because of the specific context, it cannot readily be mapped on to the Frascati definitions of R&D. TRLs range from 1-9 with: TRL 1 corresponding roughly to basic research; TRLs 2-4 to applied research; TRLs 5-6 applied research/development; TRLs 7-8 to demonstration; and TRL 9 to full-scale deployment

TRIZ: Stands for the Theory of Inventive Problem Solving; method of innovation developed in Russia by Genrich Altschuller. A problem solving methodology based on logic, data and research, not intuition. It draws on the past knowledge and ingenuity of many thousands of engineers to accelerate the project team's ability to solve problems creatively.

Value Innovation: Value Innovation is the search for new, radically different value curves. It is an eclectic mix that integrates different ideas from different sources in order to deliver higher customer value. Value innovation focuses on making the competition irrelevant by creating a leap of value for buyers and for the company, thereby opening up new and uncontested market space.

Venturepreneur: An entrepreneur building a high-risk-high-return venture around a new-to-the-world product or service.

Venture Capital: Money used to support new or unusual business ventures that exhibit above-average growth rates, significant potential for market expansion and are in need of additional financing to sustain growth or further research and development; equity or venture financing traditionally provided at the commercialization stage, increasingly available prior to commercialisation.

Reference List for Added Reading

Wolcott, Robert C. and Lippitz, Michael J. (2009). Grow From Within: Mastering Corporate Entrepreneurship and Innovation. New York: McGraw-Hill.

Gertner, Jon (2013). The Idea Factory: Bell Labs and the Great Age of American Innovation. New York: Penguin Books.

Morris, Michael H., Kuratko, Donald F., Covin, Jeffrey G. (2016). Corporate Entrepreneurship & Innovation, 3rd. Edition. Boston: South-Western College Publishing.

Collins, Jim (2001). Good to Great: Why Some Companies make the Leap...And Others Don't, 1st Edition. New York: HarperBusiness.

Vance, Ashlee (2015). Elton Musk: Tesla, SpaceX, and the Quest for a Fantastic Future. New York: Ecco Press (HarperCollins).

Taylor, Daniel (2015). The Secrets of Big Business Innovation: An insider's guide to delivering innovation, change, and growth (Kindle Edition). London: Harriman House.

Brands, Robert F. and Kleinman, Martin J. (2010). Robert's Rules of Innovation: A 10-Step Program for Corporate Survival, 1st Edition. New York: Wiley.

Jones, Terry (2012). ON Innovation: Turning ON Innovation in your culture, teams, and organization. New York: Essential Ideas, Inc.

Burgelman, Robert A. (1988). Inside Corporate Innovation: Strategy, Structure, and Managerial Skills (Reprint Edition). New York: Free Press.

Catmull, Ed and Wallace, Amy (2014). Creativity, Inc.: Overcoming the Unseen Forces That Stand in the Way of True Inspiration, 1st Edition. New York: Random House.

Keeley, Larry, Walters, Helen, Pikkel, Ryan, and Quinn, Brian (2013). Ten Types of Innovation: The Discipline of Building Breakthroughs. New York: Wiley.

How to order or download current copies of the Baldrige Criteria

Criteria for Performance Excellence

Baldrige National Quality Program

National Institute of Standards and Technology

Administration Building, Room A600

100 Bureau Drive, Stop 1020

Gaithersburg, MD 20899-1020

E-mail: nqp@nist.gov

Web address: http://www.quality.nist.gov

Notes

1. Gertner, Jon (February 2, 2016) "True Innovation" (Sunday Review) New York Times [On Line]. Retrieved from the World Wide Web: http://www.nytimes.com/2012/02/26 opinion/Sunday/innovation-and-the-bell-labs-miracle.html, p.1.

2. Fallows, James (February 2, 2016) "The 50 Greatest Breakthroughs Since the Wheel" The Atlantic [On Line]. Retrieved from the World Wide Web: http://www.theatlantic.com/magazine/archive/2013/11 /innovations-list/309536/, pp. 4-10.

3. Andrews, Evan (February 2, 2016) "History Lists: 11 Innovations that Changed History" [On Line] Retrieved from the World Wide Web: http://www.history.com/news/history-lists/11-innovations-that-changed-history. pp.) "History Lists: 11 Innovations that Changed History" [On Line] Retrieved from the World Wide Web: http://www.history.com/news/history-lists/11-innovations-that-changed-history, p. 2.

4. Andrews, Evan (February 2, 2016) "History Lists: 11 Innovations that Changed History" [On Line] Retrieved from the World Wide Web: http://www.history.com/news/history-lists/11-innovations-that-changed-history. pp.) "History Lists: 11 Innovations that Changed History" [On Line] Retrieved from the World Wide Web: http://www.history.com/news/history-lists/11-innovations-that-changed-history. pp. 2-14.

5. "Bell Labs" Wikipedia [On Line]. Retrieved from the World Wide Web: https://en.wikipedia.org/wiki/bell , p. 1.

6. Legro, Michelle (February 15, 2016) "The Idea Factory: Insights on Creativity from Bell Labs and the Golden Age of Innovation" [On Line] Retrieved from the World Wide Web: https://www.brainpickings.org/2012/03/28/the-idea-factory=bell-labs/ , pp. 3-6.

7. Carpenter, Hutch (February 15, 2016) "What Bell Labs Taught Us about Innovation" [On Line] Retrieved from the World Wide Web: http://www.innovationexcellence.com/blog/2014/01/18/what-bell-labs-taught-us-about-innovation , pp. 1-2.

8. Carpenter, Hutch (February 15, 2016) "What Bell Labs Taught Us about Innovation" [On Line] Retrieved from the World Wide Web: http://www.innovationexcellence.com/blog/2014/01/18/what-bell-labs-taught-us-about-innovation , pp. 2-7.

9. Blank, Steve (February 18, 2016) "The Future of Corporate Innovation and Entrepreneurship" [On Line] Retrieved from the World Wide Web: http://steveblank.com/2012/12/03/the-future-of-corporate-innovation-and-entrepreneurship/ , pp. 1-2.

10. Blank, Steve (February 18, 2016) "The Future of Corporate Innovation and Entrepreneurship" [On Line] Retrieved from the World Wide Web: http://steveblank.com/2012/12/03/the-future-of-corporate-innovation-and-entrepreneurship/ , p. 4.

11. Blank, Steve (February 18, 2016) "The Future of Corporate Innovation and Entrepreneurship" [On Line] Retrieved from the World Wide Web: http://steveblank.com/2012/12/03/the-future-of-corporate-innovation-and-entrepreneurship/ , p. 1.

12. Blank, Steve (February 18, 2016) "The Future of Corporate Innovation and Entrepreneurship" [On Line] Retrieved from the World Wide Web: http://steveblank.com/2012/12/03/the-future-of-corporate-innovation-and-entrepreneurship/ , p. 5.

13. Leavitt, Paige (February 18, 2016) "Rewarding Innovation" [On Line Search], p. 1.

14. Leavitt, Paige (February 18, 2016) "Rewarding Innovation" [On Line Search], p.1.

15. Phillips, Jeffrey (February 14, 2016) "Why Business Model Innovation is so Compelling" [On Line] Retrieved from the World Wide Web: http://www.innovationexcellence.com/blog/2016/02/14/why-business-model-innovation-is...., pp. 1-2.

16. Phillips, Jeffrey (February 14, 2016) "Why Business Model Innovation is so Compelling" [On Line] Retrieved from the World Wide Web: http://www.innovationexcellence.com/blog/2016/02/14/why-business-model-innovation-is.... , p 2.

17. Accenture Management Consulting (February 14, 2016) "Corporate Innovation Is Within Reach: Nurturing and Enabling an Entrepreneurial Culture (A 2013 study of US companies and their entrepreneurial cultures), pp. 2-5.

18. Bellinger, Nate (February 18, 2016) "Humana Exec on the Ups and Downs of Innovation Programs" [On Line] Retrieved from the World Wide Web: https://www.innovationleader.com/humana-exex-on-the-unvarnished-ups-and-downs-of-co.., pp. 1-2

19. Bellinger, Nate (February 18, 2016) "Humana Exec on the Ups and Downs of Innovation Programs" [On Line] Retrieved from the World Wide Web: https://www.innovationleader.com/humana-exex-on-the-unvarnished-ups-and-downs-of-co..., pp. 1-2

20. Bellinger, Nate (February 18, 2016) "Humana Exec on the Ups and Downs of Innovation Programs" [On Line] Retrieved from the World Wide Web: https://www.innovationleader.com/humana-exex-on-the-unvarnished-ups-and-downs-of-co..., pp. 1-2

21. NIST, Baldrige National Quality Program Criteria for Performance Excellence. Gaithersburg, MD: National Institute of Standards and Technology.

22. NIST, Baldrige National Quality Program Criteria for Performance Excellence. Gaithersburg, MD: National Institute of Standards and Technology.

23. NIST, Baldrige National Quality Program Criteria for Performance Excellence. Gaithersburg, MD: National Institute of Standards and Technology.

24. Leadership (Category 1) has been rewritten and revised for an Organizational assessment of corporate innovation and simplified based on Baldrige National Quality Program Criteria for Performance Excellence.

25. Strategic Planning (Category 2) has been rewritten and revised for an Organizational assessment of corporate innovation and simplified based on Baldrige National Quality Program Criteria for Performance Excellence.

26. Customer Focus (Category 3) has been rewritten and revised for an Organizational assessment of corporate innovation and simplified based on Baldrige National Quality Program Criteria for Performance Excellence.

27. Measurement, Analysis, and Knowledge Management (Category 4) has been rewritten and revised for an Organizational assessment of corporate innovation and simplified based on Baldrige National Quality Program Criteria for Performance Excellence.

28. Workforce Focus (Category 5) has been rewritten and revised for an Organizational assessment of corporate intelligence and simplified based on Baldrige National Quality Program Criteria for Performance Excellence.

29. Process Management (Category 6) has been rewritten and revised for an Organizational assessment of corporate innovation and simplified based on Baldrige National Quality Program Criteria for Performance Excellence.

30. Results (Category 7) has been rewritten and revised for an Organizational assessment of corporate innovation and simplified based on Baldrige National Quality Program Criteria for Performance Excellence.

31. Global Reporting Initiative (GRI) framework (www.globalreporting.org) was used as a model to develop the Corporate Innovation (CI) Sustainability Index.

32. NIST, Baldrige National Quality Program Criteria for Performance Excellence. Gaithersburg, MD: National Institute of Standards and Technology.

33. "Glossary of Innovation Terms" [On Line]. Retrieved from the World Wide Web: http://www.innovarsity.com/coach/glossary.html. Pp. 1-3.

Index

239

About the Author

Donald C. Fisher, Ph.D.

Donald Fisher, Executive Director/CEO of the Mid-South Quality / Productivity Center — The Quality Center is a Partnership between the Greater Memphis Chamber and Southwest Tennessee Community College and a Tennessee Board of Regents (TBR) Center of Quality Emphasis. Dr. Fisher has presented the Malcolm Baldrige Award Criteria internationally to Hitachi, Ltd. in Japan. He has also consulted with officials from the Venezuelan Ministry of Development who have reviewed adopting the Malcolm Baldrige Criteria as a model for their National Quality Award. He has worked as a visiting scholar (Commissioned by the World Bank) with the President and Prime Minister of Mauritius (an island nation located in the Indian Ocean) to oversee that nation's first ever Baldrige award program. In addition, he worked with the Federal Express Corporation in Dubai, United Arab Emirates, on their Baldrige Application for the Dubai Quality Award. He has worked with 85 presidents of worldwide companies owned by the Hong Leong management group in Kuala Lumpur, Malaysia to help them use Baldrige criteria for strategic planning. Fisher also served as an advisor for Gate Gourmet International (a division of SwissAir) "Global Service Excellence" Baldrige project in Zurich, Switzerland. Fisher is a multi-year veteran of the Board of Examiners for the prestigious Malcolm Baldrige National Quality Award and has judged quality performance based on the Baldrige criteria for more than 170 leading organizations worldwide. He has traveled throughout the world helping organizations with awards similar to the Baldrige Award. He is the author or co-author of a number of books, including The Simplified Baldrige Award Organization Assessment, Demystifying Baldrige, Measuring Up to the Baldrige, Baldrige on Campus, The Baldrige Workbook for Healthcare, Homeland Security Assessment Manual (A Comprehensive Organizational Assessment Based on Baldrige Criteria) and Corporate Sustainability Planning Assessment Guide (A Comprehensive Organizational Assessment aligned with the Global Reporting Initiative-GRI-Index). His most recent books entitled Corporate Intelligence and Corporate University are based on Baldrige Criteria for Performance Excellence. In addition, he has served on numerous quality boards throughout the United States and the World.

He has served as a judge for the Arizona State Quality Award and was a founding member of the board of directors and one of six judges for the Tennessee Quality Award. He is a past member of the Advisory Board and is presently serving on the Panel of Judges for the Commonwealth of Kentucky Quality Award and has served as both a director and judge for the Greater Memphis Award for Quality. In addition to these appointments, he was appointed to serve on the President's Quality award Program Panel of Judges in Washington D.C. and was selected as one of eight senior judges for the Secretary of the Air Force Unit Quality Award and served as one of six national Judges for the Secretary of Veterans Affairs Robert W. Carey Performance Excellence Award. He served as a consultant to the National Association of College and University Business Officers (NACUBO) National Project on developing its Baldrige-based Management Achievement Award (MAA) for American colleges and universities. In addition he served seven years as a judge for the RIT/USA Today Quality Cup Team Award.

Fisher's credentials for writing this book include spending over 25 years using Baldrige Criteria to conduct organizational assessments of various national and global organizations and reviewing innovative and entrepreneural corporate practices within such organizations as FedEx Corporation, Volvo-GM Heavy Truck Corporation, Cargill Sweeteners, Bama Companies, Hong Leong Corporation and St. Jude Children's Research Hospital.

Fisher has developed an innovative Baldrige-based corporate training system known as Process Activated Training System® (PATS), which is used by the United States Postal Service (USPS) nationwide. This system has been used to transform best innovative work practices into training scripts. Learn more about PATS at www.Processactivatedtraining.com. Dr. Fisher may be contacted via email at dfisher@memphischamber.com or by telephone at 901-543-3551.

Made in the USA
San Bernardino, CA
18 May 2016